Joanna -
Page 26
Andy
Tom

THE WORDS OF
EXTRAORDINARY
WOMEN

ALSO IN THE
NEWMARKET "WORDS OF" SERIES

The Words of Gandhi
Selected and Introduced by
Sir Richard Attenborough

The Words of Martin Luther King, Jr.
Selected and Introduced by
Coretta Scott King

The Words of Albert Schweitzer
Selected and Introduced by
Norman Cousins

The Words of Desmond Tutu
Selected and Introduced by
Naomi Tutu

The Words of Abraham Lincoln
Selected and Introduced by
Larry Shapiro

*The Words of Peace: Selections from the Speeches of the Winners of
the Nobel Peace Prize*
Selected and Edited by
Irwin Abrams

THE WORDS OF
EXTRAORDINARY
WOMEN

Selected and
Introduced by
Carolyn Warner

Foreword by
Justice Sandra Day O'Connor

Newmarket Press
New York

The Newmarket "Words Of" Series

This book is published in the United States of America and Canada.

ISBN 978-1-55704-857-8 (paperback) 10 9 8 7 6 5 4 3 2
ISBN 978-1-55704-856-1 (hardcover) 10 9 8 7 6 5 4 3 2

Library of Congress Cataloging-in-Publication Data

The words of extraordinary women / selected and introduced by Carolyn Warner; foreword by Sandra Day O'Connor.
    p. cm.
  Includes index.
  ISBN 978-1-55704-857-8 (pbk. : alk. paper) -- ISBN 978-1-55704-856-1 (hardcover : alk. paper) 1. Women--Quotations. I. Warner, Carolyn.
  HQ1233.W68 2010
  305.403--dc22

                        2010008489

QUANTITY PURCHASES
Companies, professional groups, clubs, and other organizations may qualify for special terms when ordering quantities of this title. For information, e-mail sales@newmarketpress.com; or write to Special Sales Department, Newmarket Press, 18 East 48th Street, New York, NY 10017; call (212) 832-3575 ext. 19 or 1-800-669-3903; fax (212) 832-3629.

Manufactured in the United States of America

www.newmarketpress.com

For more information about Carolyn Warner, please visit her website at **www.CarolynWarner.com**.

CONTENTS

FOREWORD

BY JUSTICE SANDRA DAY O'CONNOR

In any good speech or article the author inevitably looks for some good quotes from others which will help make the speaker's or author's points. No good presentation is without a few good quotes. In this book by Carolyn Warner we have a new resource. Carolyn has assembled a book of quotations from a number of interesting women. I am delighted to have this new resource available.

Many of the quotes are from women who are well known or famous. Some are from women who are not well known. But in these pages we can find quotations that are laugh-out-loud funny, quotations that reflect the joy of life or the pain of loss, some that make a point with words that are as subtle as a hammer and others that are as gentle as the brush of a feather. Some will make you think and some will make you wonder. But however they affect you, taken as a whole, they will provide you with a wonderful compendium of thoughts, ideas, musings, and miscellany.

If you can't find something in this book to express the point you want to make or the sentiment you want to express, my suggestion to you is to think about it, write that idea yourself, and then send it to Carolyn, because I am quite sure that she is already working on another book!

We are all indebted to Carolyn Warner for giving us such a lively resource to help each of us express ourselves with the assistance of so many women.

INTRODUCTION

BY CAROLYN WARNER

I wish that I had an exciting or mysterious story to tell about my fascination with quotations. For instance that, as a little girl, I had been visited by the ghost of John Bartlett (he of *Familiar Quotations* fame), who told me that I was destined to carry on his work. But that didn't happen. Or that I found a bottle, washed up on the seashore, containing a cryptic saying which I've spent the rest of my life trying to track down. Nice idea, but since Oklahoma is a long way from any large body of water with a tide, that didn't happen either.

The truth is much more prosaic. When I was thirteen years old, because of my late father's political connections, I became a "stump speaker" for three Oklahoma political legends—U.S. Senators Robert Kerr and Elmer Thomas and Governor Roy Turner. This was rural Oklahoma, after all, and evidently having a teenage girl with a remarkably deep voice and a flair for the dramatic was a pretty unusual draw for a political rally. The crowds must have liked it. The candidates evidently did. And I was hooked.

I then had the good fortune to have a wonderful mentor— C. E. "Pop" Grady—who was one of the finest people and best teachers I've ever had. He introduced me to debate at Classen High School, in Oklahoma City, and I was hooked again. As I quickly learned, whether you're a speaker or a debater, quotations—whether profound or pithy—are your stock in trade. You used them to prove or support or defend the point you were debating—or to disprove or attack the point of your opponents.

The more quotations you had, the better. So I began amassing quotations, laboriously copied onto 3 x 5 index cards and cataloged by topic. I still have many of those cards, now so yellowed and brittle that they could qualify as archaeological specimens. And those little 3 x 5 cards were the basis of a collection that now exceeds 40,000 quotations. As the great humorist Dave Barry (not a woman, alas) wrote, "There's a fine line between a hobby and madness." My children are firmly convinced that I crossed the line years ago!

But for more years than I'm willing to admit, my collection of quotations has served me well: as a youngster in radio and television, in high school and college debate, in business, in public office, and on the national platform speaking circuit, I've never stopped using and collecting them.

And, to this day, I've never found a better way to enhance the communications process than by reinforcing the points or concepts I wish to make with timely, memorable quotations from someone whose life, actions, character, fame, or notoriety makes whatever they have to say worth repeating.

Quotations are able to illustrate in a few words what is difficult to explain in many. Whether you are speaking or writing, collaborating or motivating, sharing or leading, quotations can be used to:

- *validate* your own point of view;
- *vary* the pace of remarks, whether from the platform or at the conference table;
- *reinforce* a salient point;
- *demonstrate* that a mind greater than yours has also expressed your position;
- *illustrate* a thought in a way that you alone might not be able to easily express;
- *evoke emotions* that you might not be able to arouse in your own words;

- *establish a common bond* with your listeners or readers by quoting a person known and respected;
- *inject humor* when it might be needed most.

Collecting quotations might not carry the same excitement quotient as climbing Camelback Mountain, but it is considerably easier. No newspaper, magazine, journal, book, letter, pamphlet, advertisement, or speech has been safe from my ready pen and 3 x 5 cards. A good quotation may appear when and where you least expect it. I find them in the writings of both the famous and the infamous. I have found some of the best in poems sent to me by schoolchildren, in conversations with interesting people, in speeches I have heard, and in business periodicals that have never pretended to be repositories of quotable quotes.

What keeps me in pursuit of just the right quotation is that I use them now for the same purposes I used them in my youth: to support positions, to entertain, to provoke thought, to enlighten, to illustrate a point, to use the eloquence and wisdom of great—or at least quotable—women and men to validate in their words the points or principles I want to express.

Two things about a good quotation fascinate me:

- *Its universality.* The wise words of an elementary school teacher can be the perfect illustration to use in a roomful of bankers.
- *Its timeless quality.* A bit of wisdom uttered in the thirties by a farm woman in the Oklahoma Dust Bowl is still the best piece of career-planning advice I've ever come across.

In assembling my collection of quotations, and in putting together the material for this book, I have focused exclusively on the words of women. Why? Because, as a woman, and as a woman speaker, writer, and advocate, I believe I have something of an obligation to help enlarge the voices of other women—famous women, women far wiser and more accomplished than I am, and women who are utterly unknown.

I also found out the hard way, many years ago, that there was an absence of a usable source of quotations by women. It is my goal to help close that gap. In this process—compiling the words of both celebrated and uncelebrated women for this book—I have tried to document the birth and death dates, nationality, and profession of each, which are listed in the back of this book in the biographical index.

The quotations in this book are divided into eleven topic areas. My selection of both quotations and topic areas was purely arbitrary. It was most assuredly not an exercise in objectivity. I selected the topics because I believe they are of particular interest and applicability to women. I selected the quotations because I like them.

The reader will note that the topic areas are essentially positive in nature. There isn't a chapter on "War," for instance. Or on "Hate." (There isn't one on "Men," either, but that's another story.) This isn't because of some Pollyanna-ish worldview, but because my own personal philosophy is that life is too short to focus on the negative. We have to admit the reality of the negative, certainly, but we do not have to focus on it. Doing so colors our day and our life in ways that are simply not productive.

It is my fond hope that these quotations and their topic areas will form a basic library for women, whether writers, speakers, thinkers, or just plain readers. I hope that every woman who uses this book will be motivated to start her own collection of quotable quotes, her own assemblage of words that motivate, inform, inspire, challenge, entertain, and validate.

But if you can, try to stay on the "hobby" side of that line. Enjoy!

1

THE ARTS

"Art is about the pilgrimage from appearance to reality."
—IRIS MURDOCH

The *arts* have been called the "objectification of feeling and the subjectification of nature."

The first time I read those words, I simply read them, as words, gazed off into space, and thought I had just read a masterpiece of "doublespeak." Then I read them again, thinking carefully this time about how one might actually quantify impressions or feelings, or how one could transform the visual or the physical into lasting mental pictures.

Slowly, images of great paintings and passages of great writing, visions of beautiful places and snatches of beautiful music came to mind. They were there the whole time, right between my ears. From the transcendent beauty of a Monet landscape to the aural charm of the thunderstorm in Beethoven's "Pastoral" Symphony to Thoreau's description of Walden Pond, nature entered my mind as surely as if I were seeing, hearing, or reading these great representations of nature.

And so it is with people. No matter how flawed, what each person has done in her life represents a piece of art.

A great teacher brings to the classroom a set of perceptions, talents, and skills that enables her to stimulate creative thinking in her students. A successful businesswoman brings to the job a set of qualities unique to her. Just as an artist paints upon a canvas using a chosen palette of colors, so do we, as people, build a life that is a composite of our "colors"—our character, our talents, our bright and dark spots.

I love quotations about the arts—spoken, written, painted, sculpted, read, or sung—because I believe that art in all its forms represents manifestations of our belief in tomorrow: someone will be here to see the painting or the desert vista, to read or hear the words, to dance the dance and hum the notes after their creators are gone, just as we enjoy today the creations of past generations. I see the arts as vehicles that enable the present to communicate with the future.

I have chosen to include a chapter of quotations about the arts because we simply cannot reach toward tomorrow or learn from the past if we lack an appreciation of what transcends the moment. The arts, and even words about the arts, are always there to elevate our spirits.

THE ARTS

"A bird does not sing because he has an answer. He sings because he has a song."

—*JOAN WALSH ANGLUND*

"To look backward for a while is to refresh the eye, to restore it, and to render it the more fit for its prime function of looking forward."

—*MARGARET FAIRLESS BARBER*

"A photograph can be an instant of life captured for eternity that will never cease looking back at you."

—*BRIGITTE BARDOT*

"Imagination has always had powers of resurrection that no science can match."

—*INGRID BENGIS*

"Life begets life. Energy creates energy. It is by spending oneself that one becomes rich."

—*SARAH BERNHARDT*

"Cease to be a drudge, seek to be an artist."

—*MARY MCLEOD BETHUNE*

"There are sounds to seasons. There are sounds to places and there are sounds to every time in one's life."

—ALISON WYRLEY BIRCH

"Order is a lovely thing;
On disarray it lays its wing,
Teaching simplicity to sing."

—ANNA BRANCH

"But he that dares not grasp the thorn
Should never crave the rose."

—ANNE BRONTË

"Neither birth nor sex forms a limit to genius."

—CHARLOTTE BRONTË

"The lessons taught in great books are misleading. The commerce in life is rarely so simple and never so just."

—ANITA BROOKNER

"Every actor has a natural animosity towards every other actor, present or absent, living or dead."

—LOUISE BROOKS

"Those who contemplate the beauty of the earth find reserves of strength that will endure as long as life lasts."

—RACHEL CARSON

"Art is good when it springs from necessity. This kind of origin is the guarantee of its value; there is no other."

—ANGELA CARTER

"Treat your friends as you do your pictures, and place them in their best light."

—*JENNIE JEROME CHURCHILL*

"I write from my knowledge, not my lack, from my strength, not my weakness. I am not interested if anyone knows whether or not I am familiar with big words, I am interested in trying to render big ideas in a simple way. I am interested in being understood."

—*LUCILLE CLIFTON*

"Creativity is inventing, experimenting, growing, taking risks, making mistakes and having fun."

—*MARY LOU COOK*

"The truest expression of a people is in its dance and its music. Bodies never lie."

—*AGNES DE MILLE*

"Art is why I get up in the morning, but my definition ends there. You know, I don't think it's fair that I'm living for something I can't even define."

—*ANI DIFRANCO*

"Only after the writer lets literature shape her, can she, perhaps, shape literature."

—*ANNIE DILLARD*

"The artist is the only lover. He alone has the pure vision of beauty: and love is the vision of the soul when it is permitted to gaze upon immortal beauty."

—ISADORA DUNCAN

"I think that real beauty exists where we least expect it, in an unrevealed sense, disclosing itself only as we earnestly search for it, thus stimulating our creative faculties."

—JESSIE BENTON EVANS

"I have never been contained except I made the prison."

—MARI EVANS

"Through books, ideas find their way to human brains, and ideals to human hearts and souls."

—DOROTHY CANFIELD FISHER

"Just don't give up on trying to do what you really want to do. Where there is love and inspiration, I don't think you can go wrong."

—ELLA FITZGERALD

"If I have learnt anything, it is that life forms no logical patterns. It is haphazard and full of beauties which I try to catch as they fly by, for who knows whether any of them will ever return?"

—MARGOT FONTEYN

"When a man gets up to speak, people listen, then look. When a woman gets up, people look; then if they like what they see, they listen."

—*PAULINE FREDERICK*

"Comedy is essentially a miracle. I believe I'm as important to society as a doctor; to create laughter creates magic. These days nothing is more important."

—*KATHLEEN FREEMAN*

"To be surrounded by beautiful things has much influence upon the human creature. To make beautiful things has more."

—*CHARLOTTE PERKINS GILMAN*

"The body says what words cannot."

—*MARTHA GRAHAM*

"We must overcome the notion that we must be regular. It robs you of the chance to be extraordinary and leads you to the mediocre."

—*UTA HAGEN*

"I love inscriptions on flyleaves and notes in margins. I like the comradely sense of turning pages someone else turned, and reading passages someone long gone has called my attention to."

—*HELENE HANFF*

"Fantasies are more than substitutes for unpleasant reality; they are also dress rehearsals, plans. All acts performed in the world begin in the imagination."
—*BARBARA GRIZZUTI HARRISON*

"I do believe it is possible to create, even without ever writing a word or painting a picture, by simply molding one's inner life. And that too is a deed."
—*ETTY HILLESUM*

"No two people on earth are alike, and it's got to be that way in music or it isn't music."
—*BILLIE HOLIDAY*

"Beauty is in the eye of the beholder."
—*MARGARET HUNGERFORD*

"Art is the window to man's soul. Without it, he would never be able to see beyond his immediate world; nor could the world see the man within."
—*LADY BIRD JOHNSON*

"I do not want to die until I have faithfully made the most of my talent and cultivated the seed that was placed in me until the last small twig has grown."
—*KÄTHE KOLLWITZ*

"There have been great societies that did not use the wheel, but there have been no societies that did not tell stories."
—*URSULA K. LEGUIN*

"It is easy for a designer to create unusual and amusing new clothes with a certain shock value. The difficulty is restraint."
—*IRENE LENTZ*

"I believe that true identity is found in creative activity springing from within. It is found, paradoxically, when one loses oneself. Woman can best re-find herself by losing herself in some kind of creative activity of her own."
—*ANNE MORROW LINDBERGH*

"There is a fountain of youth: it is your mind, your talents, the creativity you bring to your life and the lives of the people you love."
—*SOPHIA LOREN*

"They say the movies should be more like life. I think life should be more like the movies."
—*MYRNA LOY*

"I think of life itself now as a wonderful play that I've written for myself, and so my purpose is to have the utmost fun playing my part."
—*SHIRLEY MACLAINE*

"Had she paints, or clay, or knew the discipline of dance, or strings; had she anything to engage her tremendous curiosity and her gift for metaphor, she might have exchanged the restlessness and preoccupation with whim for any activity that provided her with all she yearned for. And like any artist with no art form, she became dangerous."
—*TONI MORRISON*

"I look back on my life like a good day's work; it was done and I am satisfied with it."
                —GRANDMA MOSES (ANNA MARY ROBERTSON MOSES)

"Friendship is an art, and very few persons are born with a natural gift for it."
                                                —KATHLEEN NORRIS

"Singing has always seemed to me the most perfect means of expression. It is so spontaneous. Since I cannot sing, I paint."
                                                —GEORGIA O'KEEFFE

"Although one may fail to find happiness in theatrical life, one never wishes to give it up after having once tasted its fruits."
                                                —ANNA PAVLOVA

"My fiction is reportage, only I do something to it; I arrange it and it is fiction, but it happened."
                                                —KATHERINE ANNE PORTER

"I read and walked for miles at night along the beach, writing bad blank verse and searching endlessly for someone wonderful who would step out of the darkness and change my life. It never crossed my mind that that person could be me."
                                                —ANNA QUINDLEN

"Poetry is a subconscious conversation. It is as much the work of those who understand it as those who make it."

—*SONIA SANCHEZ*

"I always have a quotation for everything—it saves original thinking."

—*DOROTHY L. SAYERS*

"And it came to pass that after a time the artist was forgotten, but the work lived."

—*OLIVE SCHREINER*

"You will jump to it someday. Then you'll fly. You'll really fly. After that you'll quite simply, quite calmly make your own stones, your own floor plan, your own sound."

—*ANNE SEXTON*

"My imagination, unbidden, possessed and guided me."

—*MARY SHELLEY*

"Wit consists of knowing the resemblance of things which differ and the difference of things which are alike."

—*MADAME DE STAËL*

"The soul is the fire that darts its rays through all the senses; it is in this fire that existence consists; all the observations and all the efforts of the philosophers ought to turn towards this, the center and moving power of our sentiments and our ideas."

—*MADAME DE STAËL*

"Career is too pompous a word. It was a job, and I have always felt privileged to be paid for what I love doing."

—*BARBARA STANWYCK*

"I want to dance always, to be good and not evil, and when it is all over not to have the feeling that I might have done better."

—*RUTH ST. DENIS*

"Put blinders on to those things that conspire to hold you back, especially the ones in your own head. Guard your good mood. Listen to music every day, joke, and love, and read more for fun, especially poetry."

—*MERYL STREEP*

"If anything at all, perfection is finally attained not when there is no longer anything to add but when there is no longer anything to take away."

—*MARIA TALLCHIEF*

"With writing, you hear voices and give yourself over to them and they become flesh and blood by putting pen to paper. With acting, the voices become flesh and blood through the instrument of your body. Either way, it's mysticism that I'm interested in."

—*REGINA TAYLOR*

"To a historian, libraries are food, shelter and even muse."
—BARBARA TUCHMAN

"Helped are those who create anything at all, for they shall relive the thrill of their own conception and realize a partnership in the creation of the Universe that keeps them responsible and cheerful."
—ALICE WALKER

"A work of art has an author and yet, when it is perfect, it has something which is essentially anonymous about it."
—SIMONE WEIL

"It had been startling and disappointing to me to find out that story books had been written by people, that books were not natural wonders, coming up of themselves like grass."
—EUDORA WELTY

"I always say, keep a diary and someday it'll keep you."
—MAE WEST

"Silence may be as variously shaded as speech."
—EDITH WHARTON

"Imagination! Who can sing thy force?
Or who describe the swiftness of thy course?"
　　　　　　　　　　　—*PHYLLIS WHEATLEY*

"The beauty of the world has two edges, one of laughter, one
of anguish, cutting the heart asunder."
　　　　　　　　　　　—*VIRGINIA WOOLF*

2

CHARACTER

*"I cannot and will not cut my conscience
to fit this year's fashion."*
—LILLIAN HELLMAN

My dictionary defines *character* as the "complex of mental and ethical traits marking a person, group, or nation." It also speaks of character as "moral excellence and firmness." I think that sums it up pretty well.

There is also another element to character that I think is important: each of us must create or define our own character.

For me, this process is best defined by following the advice that I first got many years ago from my grandmother, Nellie Hershey Tullis. She was an Oklahoma farm woman, so her philosophy was often expressed in agricultural or farming terms. And what she said about character was:

Plant a thought, reap an act;
Plant an act, reap a habit;
Plant a habit, reap a character;
Plant a character, reap a destiny.

As a little girl, I thought those were just some words from an old lady. Only as I've gotten older and, hopefully, smarter, have I come to realize that what Grandmother was trying to give me was, essentially, a recipe for life. Our thoughts are often converted into action; repeated actions eventually do become habits; the composite of all these mental and spiritual habits comprise our character.

I have also heard it put more succinctly: your character is your deliberate creation of yourself.

Over the years, I have found that what women have had to say about character has been both helpful and instructive to me. These quotations are a distillation of that instruction.

CHARACTER

"It is not in the still calm of life, or the repose of a pacific station, that great characters are formed. Great necessities call out great virtues."

—*ABIGAIL ADAMS*

"Do not do what you would undo if caught."

—*LEAH ARENDT*

"There is no charm equal to tenderness of heart."

—*JANE AUSTEN*

"You don't get to choose how you're going to die. Or when. You can only decide how you're going to live."

—*JOAN BAEZ*

"You grow up the day you have the first real laugh—at yourself."

—*ETHEL BARRYMORE*

"It's best to have failure happen early in life. It wakes up the Phoenix bird in you so you rise from the ashes."

—*ANNE BAXTER*

"We grow neither better nor worse as we get old, but more like ourselves."

—*MAY LAMBERTON BECKER*

"Being nice should never be perceived as being weak. It's not a sign of weakness, it's a sign of courtesy, manners, grace, a woman's ability to make everyone feel at home, and it should never be construed as weakness."
—*BENAZIR BHUTTO*

"Justice is better than chivalry if we cannot have both."
—*ALICE STONE BLACKWELL*

"Courage is often merely the result of despair. We cease to fear when we have ceased to hope."
—*LADY BLESSINGTON (MARGUERITE POWER GARDINER)*

"What we suffer, what we endure, is done by us, as individuals, in private."
—*LOUISE BOGAN*

"Flattery is so necessary to all of us that we flatter one another just to be flattered in return."
—*MARJORIE BOWEN*

"Youth is the time of getting, middle age of improving, and old age of spending."
—*ANNE BRADSTREET*

"Let the world know you as you are, not as you think you should be, because sooner or later, if you are posing, you will forget the pose, and then where are you?"
—*FANNY BRICE*

"The price of dishonesty is self-destruction."
—*RITA MAE BROWN*

"Standing as I do, in the view of God and eternity, I realise that patriotism is not enough. I must have no hatred or bitterness towards anyone."
—*EDITH CAVELL*

"Love is the big booming beat which covers up the noise of hate."
—*MARGARET CHO*

"It is necessary to try to surpass one's self always; this occupation ought to last as long as life."
—*QUEEN CHRISTINA*

"One is forever throwing away substance for shadows."
—*JENNIE JEROME CHURCHILL*

"The truth is that the historical and current condition of you and yours is rooted in slavery, is shaped by it, is bound to it, and is the reality against which all else must be gauged."
—*JOHNETTA B. COLE*

"I measure every Grief I meet,
With narrow, probing, Eyes—
I wonder if It weighs like Mine—
Or has an Easier size."

—*EMILY DICKINSON*

"You can't test courage cautiously."

—*ANNIE DILLARD*

"Please know that I am aware of the hazards. I want to do it because I want to do it. Women must try to do things as men have tried. When they fail, their failure must be a challenge to others."

—*AMELIA EARHART*

"In youth we learn; in age we understand."

—*MARIE EBNER-ESCHENBACH*

"Learn to be quiet enough to hear the sound of the genuine within yourself so that you can hear it in other people."

—*MARIAN WRIGHT EDELMAN*

"Childhood is only the beautiful and happy time in contemplation and retrospect: to the child it is full of deep sorrows, the meaning of which is unknown."

—*GEORGE ELIOT (MARY ANN EVANS)*

"Our deeds will travel with us from afar, and what we have been makes us what we are."

—*GEORGE ELIOT (MARY ANN EVANS)*

"Cowards falter, but danger is often overcome by those who nobly dare."

—*QUEEN ELIZABETH I*

"The upward course of a nation's history is due in the long run to the soundness of heart of its average men and women."

—*QUEEN ELIZABETH II*

"True power, honest power, real power flows not from subordination, but collaboration and cooperation."

—*CRISTINA FERNÁNDEZ DE KIRCHNER*

"The goal is to transform data into information, and information into insight."

—*CARLY FIORINA*

"To force opinion is like pushing the magnetized needle round by brute strength until it points to where we wish the North Star stood, rather than to where it really is."

—*DOROTHY CANFIELD FISHER*

"He who has courage and faith will never perish in misery!"

—*ANNE FRANK*

"Parents can only give good advice or put them on the right paths, but the final forming of a person's character lies in their own hands."

—*ANNE FRANK*

"When she stopped conforming to the conventional picture of femininity she finally began to enjoy being a woman."

—*BETTY FRIEDAN*

"I do not have a big political organization to conduct my campaign. Nor do I have big signs nailed to trees, fences and posts to disfigure the countryside. I do not want such a campaign. My habits and desires are in keeping with my resources. They are plain and devoid of all pretenses."

—*ANA FROHMILLER*

"Part of being raised as a black child in America is developing skills to cope with and understand reality. Some of it is separating ignorance from malicious intent. If anything, it really helps you to know who you are, so you're not reactionary."

—*ANN FUDGE*

"Deafness has left me acutely aware of both the duplicity that language is capable of and the many expressions the body cannot hide."

—*TERRY GALLOWAY*

"You must learn to be still in the midst of activity and to be vibrantly alive in repose."

—*INDIRA GANDHI*

"Courage looks you straight in the eye. She is not impressed with power trippers, and she knows first aid. Courage is not afraid to weep, and she is not afraid to pray, even when she is not sure who she is praying to. When she walks it is clear she has made the journey from loneliness to solitude. The people who told me she was stern were not lying; they just forgot to mention she was kind."

—*J. RUTH GENDLER*

"Sometimes people say unkind or thoughtless things, and when they do, it is best to be a little hard of hearing—to tune out and not snap back in anger or impatience."

—*RUTH BADER GINSBURG*

"If now isn't a good time for the truth I don't see when we'll get to it."

—*NIKKI GIOVANNI*

"Idealists—foolish enough to throw caution to the winds—have advanced mankind and have enriched the world."

—*EMMA GOLDMAN*

"Courage is very important. Like a muscle, it is strengthened by use."

—*RUTH GORDON*

"Only friends will tell you the truths you need to hear to make the last part of your life bearable."

—*FRANCINE DU PLESSIX GRAY*

"I can remember walking as a child. It was not customary to say you were fatigued. It was customary to complete the goal of the expedition."

—*KATHARINE HEPBURN*

"If I could wish for my life to be perfect, it would be tempting but I would have to decline, for life would no longer teach me anything."

—*ALLYSON JONES*

"Don't compromise yourself. You are all you've got."
                                                —JANIS JOPLIN

"We live in the present. We dream of the future, but we learn eternal truths from the past."
        — MADAME CHIANG KAI-SHEK (SOONG MEI-LING)

"It seems to me that there is in each of us a capacity to comprehend the impressions and emotions which have been experienced by mankind from the beginning. This inherited capacity is a sort of sixth sense—a soul-sense which sees, hears, feels, all in one."
                                                —HELEN KELLER

"We ask ourselves why terrible obstacles should be placed in our path. We cannot but wonder at times why we cannot have smooth sailing instead of being compelled always to fight against adverse winds and rough seas. No doubt the reason is that character cannot be developed in ease and quiet. Only through experiences of trial and suffering can the soul be strengthened, vision cleared, ambition inspired, and success achieved."
                                                —HELEN KELLER

"The main thing is to care. Care very hard, even if it is only a game you are playing."
                                            —BILLIE JEAN KING

"People are like stained-glass windows. They sparkle and shine when the sun is out, but when the darkness sets in their true beauty is revealed only if there is a light from within."

—ELISABETH KÜBLER-ROSS

"Hope begins in the dark, the stubborn hope that if you just show up and try to do the right thing, the dawn will come. You wait and watch and work; you don't give up."

—ANNE LAMOTT

"The most exhausting thing in life is to be insincere."

—ANNE MORROW LINDBERGH

"Courage is the ladder on which all the other virtues mount."

—CLARE BOOTHE LUCE

"Entire communities also come to understand that while it is necessary to hold their governments accountable, it is equally important that in their own relationships with each other, they exemplify the leadership values they wish to see in their own leaders, namely justice, integrity, and trust."

—WANGARI MAATHAI

"Everything in life that we really accept undergoes a change. So suffering must become love. That is the mystery."

—KATHERINE MANSFIELD

"Honesty has come to mean the privilege of insulting you to your face without expecting redness."
— *JUDITH MARTIN ("MISS MANNERS")*

"Those who do not know how to weep with their whole heart don't know how to laugh either."
— *GOLDA MEIR*

"The world stands out on either side,
No wider than the heart is wide;
Above the world is stretched the sky,—
No higher than the soul is high.
The heart can push the sea and land,
Farther away on either hand;
The soul can split the sky in two,
And let the face of God shine through.
But East and West will pinch the heart
That cannot keep them pushed apart;
And he whose soul is flat—the sky
Will cave in on him by and by."
— *EDNA ST. VINCENT MILLAY*

"Love and the hope of it are not things one can learn; they are a part of life's heritage."
— *MARIA MONTESSORI*

"Race and gender are distractions. It's not enough you're white. It's not enough you're black. You can't rest on your victimhood or your shame or your privilege or your religion. You have nothing but you and your human response."
— *TONI MORRISON*

"The real art of conversation is not only to say the right thing in the right place but to leave unsaid the wrong thing at the tempting moment."

—*DOROTHY NEVILL*

"Stay true to yourself and never let what somebody else says distract you from your goals."

—*MICHELLE OBAMA*

"Fame has only the span of a day, they say. But to live in the hearts of the people—that is worth something."

—*OUIDA*

"Each person must live their life as a model for others."

—*ROSA PARKS*

"Old people who shine from the inside look ten to twenty years younger."

—*DOLLY PARTON*

"The forgiving state of mind is a magnetic power for attracting good. No good thing can be withheld from the forgiving state of mind."

—*CATHERINE PONDER*

"The attributes of a great lady may still be found in the rule of the Four S's: Sincerity, Simplicity, Sympathy and Serenity."

—*EMILY POST*

"I would much rather have regrets about not doing what people said, than regretting not doing what my heart led me to and wondering what life had been like if I'd just been myself."

—*BRITTANY RENEE*

"If you do things well, do them better. Be daring, be first, be different, be just."

—*ANITA RODDICK*

"If you don't stand for something, you will stand for anything."

—*GINGER ROGERS*

"A woman whose smile is open and whose expression is glad has a kind of beauty no matter what she wears."

—*ANNE ROIPHE*

"It takes a great deal of courage to stand up to your enemies, but even more to stand up to your friends."

—*J. K. ROWLING*

"The old woman I shall become will be quite different from the woman I am now. Another I is beginning."

—*GEORGE SAND (ARMANDINE AURORE LUCILE DUPIN, BARONESS DUDEVANT)*

"Woman must not accept; she must challenge. She must not be awed by that which has been built up around her; she must reverence that woman in her which struggles for expression."

—MARGARET SANGER

"Time and trouble will tame an advanced young woman, but an advanced old woman is uncontrollable by any earthly force."

—DOROTHY L. SAYERS

"You need only claim the events of your life to make yourself yours. When you truly possess all you have been and done, which may take some time, you are fierce with reality."

—FLORIDA SCOTT-MAXWELL

"My doctrine is this: that if we see cruelty or wrong that we have the power to stop, and do nothing, we make ourselves sharers in the guilt."

—ANNA SEWELL

"There can be no happiness if the things we believe in are different from the things we do."

—FREYA STARK

"Reach high, for stars lie hidden in your soul.
Dream deep, for every dream precedes the goal."
—PAMELA VAULL STARR

"Let me listen to me and not to them."
—GERTRUDE STEIN

"Integrate what you believe into every single area of your life. Take your heart to work and ask the most and best of everybody else."
—MERYL STREEP

"Courage is not the towering oak
that sees storms come and go;
it is the fragile blossom
that opens in the snow."

—ALICE M. SWAIM

"To love deeply in one direction makes us more loving in all others."
—ANNE-SOPHIE SWETCHINE

"I hate faces that have no questioning in them, no quest for wanting to learn more, look at more, see more, BE more!"
—MARIA TALLCHIEF

"All of us are human and prone to sin. Just see to it that you don't let your sins turn into bad habits."
—SAINT TERESA OF AVILA

"To those waiting with bated breath for that favourite media catch-phrase, the U-turn, I have only one thing to say, 'You turn if you want to. The lady's not turning.'"

—*MARGARET THATCHER*

"Great events make me quiet and calm; it is only trifles that irritate my nerves."

—*QUEEN VICTORIA*

"So we are not alone in seeing the need for change. We may be alone in making it. For the sake of our earth and ourselves, we must. What men value has brought us to the brink of death. What women find worthy may bring us back to life."

—*MARILYN WARING*

"I am a writer who came of a sheltered life. A sheltered life can be a daring life as well. For all daring starts from within."

—*EUDORA WELTY*

"So many gods, so many creeds,
So many paths that wind and wind,
While just the art of being kind,
Is all the sad world needs."

—*ELLA WHEELER WILCOX*

"If you do not tell the truth about yourself, you cannot tell it about other people."

—VIRGINIA WOOLF

"It is probable that both in life and in art the values of a woman are not the values of a man."

—VIRGINIA WOOLF

"It's an advantage to be pretty. You get attention without trying. But after the first five minutes, you are on your own."

—LORETTA YOUNG

3

EDUCATION

"You suddenly understand something you've understood all your life, but in a new way. That is what learning is."
—DORIS LESSING

Quotations about *education* are not just by, or for, professional educators. The topic of education, like quotations about education, is so broad that there is, literally, something for everybody.

Like so many topics in this book, I find quotations about education to be empowering. Why? Because every positive act requires that education in some form occur. Education is the process of moving—via facts, information, experience and perceptions—from ignorance to knowledge and, hopefully, to wisdom.

The fascinating thing about education is that no one can be *given* an education. All that we can be given is the opportunity to learn. What we do with that opportunity is up to us.

One of my favorite sayings about the importance of education is "What you're not up on, you're down on." True! There is no vacuum in real life. We are either instructed positively (causing us to be "up" on something) or negatively (causing us to be "down" on something). In any act of communication, one or the other will occur. Putting it plainly, nobody is ever *not* educated. Thus, the companion to education is change.

The larger truth of that "up-down" aphorism is double-edged: if we don't properly communicate with people about our purpose, we will not succeed in it—whatever "it" might be. Whether in business, politics, family life, or friendships, we bear the responsibility of educating the people with whom we interact about who we are, what we do, what we want to do, what we want them to know, and how we want them to respond. Basically, we are communicating with others so that they will be "up" on what we are "up" on. That, to me, is the essence of the educational process.

EDUCATION

"America's future will be determined by the home and the school. The child becomes largely what he is taught; hence we must watch what we teach, and how we live."

—*JANE ADDAMS*

"Perhaps I may record here my protest against the efforts, so often made, to shield children and young people from all that has to do with death and sorrow, to give them a good time at all hazards on the assumption that the ills of life will come soon enough. Young people themselves often resent this attitude on the part of their elders; they feel set aside and belittled as if they were denied the common human experiences."

—*JANE ADDAMS*

"[My mother] said that I must always be tolerant of ignorance but understanding of illiteracy. That some people unable to go to school were more educated and more intelligent than college professors."

—*MAYA ANGELOU*

"You must learn day by day, year by year, to broaden your horizon. The more things you love, the more you are interested in, the more you enjoy, the more you are indignant about—the more you have left when anything happens."

—*ETHEL BARRYMORE*

"Authority without wisdom is like a heavy ax without an edge, fitter to bruise than polish."

—*ANNE BRADSTREET*

"Beauty can't amuse you, but brainwork—reading, writing, thinking—can."

—*HELEN GURLEY BROWN*

"We learn as much from sorrow as from joy, as much from illness as from health, from handicap as from advantage—and indeed perhaps more."

—*PEARL S. BUCK*

"Good education is the essential foundation of a strong democracy."

—*BARBARA BUSH*

"My mother read me bedtime stories until I was six years old. It was a sneak attack on her part. As soon as I really got to like the stories, she said, "Here's the book, now you read."

—*OCTAVIA BUTLER*

"I was taught that the way of progress is neither swift nor easy."

—*MARIE CURIE*

"We have to talk about liberating minds as well as liberating society."

—*ANGELA DAVIS*

"We learn best to listen to our own voices if we are listening at the same time to other women—whose stories, for all our differences, turn out, if we listen well, to be our stories also."
—*BARBARA DEMING*

"Education is for improving the lives of others and for leaving your community and world better than you found it."
—*MARIAN WRIGHT EDELMAN*

"No idea is so antiquated that it was not once modern. No idea is so modern that it will not someday be antiquated."
—*ELLEN GLASGOW*

"A good finance minister knows perfectly well that in the long term a country cannot avoid investing in education and research."
—*DALIA GRYBAUSKAITE*

"Some people see education in America as the little red schoolhouse, when the skies were not cloudy all day and nobody ever heard of smog. They are practicing 'selective amnesia.' The truth of the matter is that education in America is what makes dreams come true for all students, able-bodied or not, rich or poor, whether their skin is white, yellow or black or brown or any shade of the rainbow. Education allows children to enter into the richness of the experience of the mind."
—*SHIRLEY HUFSTEDLER*

"We older women who know we aren't heroines can offer our younger sisters, at the very least, an honest report of what we have learned and how we have grown."

—*ELIZABETH JANEWAY*

"Education remains the key to both economic and political empowerment."

—*BARBARA JORDAN*

"The highest result of education is tolerance."

—*HELEN KELLER*

"Our feelings are our most genuine paths to knowledge."

—*AUDRE LORDE*

"Books are more than books, they are the life. The very heart and core of ages past, the reason why men lived and worked and died, the essence and quintessence of their lives."

—*AMY LOWELL*

"We will be victorious if we have not forgotten how to learn."

—*ROSA LUXEMBURG*

"I don't think anybody anywhere can talk about the future of their people or of an organization without talking about education. Whoever controls the education of our children controls our future."

—*WILMA MANKILLER*

"I learn, by understanding myself, to understand others."
—*KATHERINE MANSFIELD*

"I touch the future. I teach."
—*CHRISTA MCAULIFFE*

"One cannot have wisdom without living life."
—*DOROTHY MCCALL*

"There are no new truths, but only truths that have not been recognized by those who have perceived them without noticing."
—*MARY MCCARTHY*

"Children must be taught how to think, not what to think."
—*MARGARET MEAD*

"If you can't count, they can cheat you. If you can't read, they can beat you."
—*TONI MORRISON*

"Falling out of love is very enlightening; for a short while you see the world with new eyes."
—*IRIS MURDOCH*

"A master can tell you what he expects of you. A teacher, though, awakens your own expectations."
—*PATRICIA NEAL*

"It is instructive to look at history and passively ponder the past: What if? But that exercise is useless if it does not lead directly to the realization that each day is part of history, and every generation is honor-bound to use its particular range of knowledge and experience to order its priorities humanely, judiciously, ethically, effectively and efficiently."

—*ANTONIA COELLO NOVELLO*

"Wit has truth in it; wisecracking is simply calisthenics with words."

—*DOROTHY PARKER*

"Experience is what happens to you in the long run, the truth that finally overtakes you."

—*KATHERINE ANNE PORTER*

"I would be the most content if my children grew up to be the kind of people who think decorating consists mostly of building enough bookshelves."

—*ANNA QUINDLEN*

"You can achieve great things by being willing to learn new things, being able to assimilate new information quickly and being able to get along with and work with other people."

—*SALLY RIDE*

"The test of a good teacher is not how many questions he can ask his pupils that they will answer readily, but how many questions he inspires them to ask him which he finds it hard to answer."

—*ALICE WELLINGTON ROLLINS*

"A democratic form of government, a democratic way of life, presupposes free public education over a long period; it presupposes also an education for personal responsibility that too often is neglected."

—*ELEANOR ROOSEVELT*

"By looking at the questions the kids are asking, we learn the scope of what needs to be done."

—*BUFFY SAINT MARIE*

"Words are more powerful than perhaps anyone suspects, and once deeply engraved in a child's mind, they are not easily eradicated."

—*MAY SARTON*

"Education in the white man's world is enriching and essential to economic success, but it need not mean the giving up of our proud Pima heritage."

—*ANNA MOORE SHAW*

"Children require guidance and sympathy far more than instruction."

—*ANNE SULLIVAN*

"I feel sure that no girl could go to the altar, and would probably refuse, if she knew all."

—*QUEEN VICTORIA*

"Our [Navajo] children must always remain close to their parents; our parents must have a close connection to our schools; and parents and teachers must work closely together for the good of the child. This is the key to education for our Navajo children, and education is the key to the future of the Navajo people."

—*ANNIE DODGE WAUNEKA*

"We want the facts to fit the preconceptions. When they don't, it is easier to ignore the facts than to change the preconceptions."

—*JESSAMYN WEST*

4

FAITH

"Finding spiritual meaning is essential.
This is part of the way we imagine, we hope, we fear,
the way we explore. We can't live without it."
—ELAINE PAGELS

One of my favorite authors begins a bestselling book with these profound words: "Life is difficult."* Yes, it is. And making it through life, like making it through the large and small elements that make up our life, requires *faith*.

Faith has been described as the first step of a leap into the unknown. I believe this is true. I also believe that the antithesis of faith—fear, that terrible precursor to failure—is like a leap into a terrible, anticipated *known*.

I am convinced that the difference between the ultimate outcomes of those two leaps is the degree to which you can generate a feeling of faith—faith in yourself, in your principles, and in your purpose.

My personal faith and my inner sense of empowerment grow out of a belief that there is a higher power that validates who I am and confirms my worth as a human being. This is my

---

*M. Scott Peck, *The Road Less Traveled*

affirmation, and it enables me. It allows me to accept the difficulties of life as simply being a series of hurdles that can be overcome and not as impenetrable barriers.

I find the expressions of faith by other women to also be enabling, because the power of words to motivate is almost miraculous. No matter by what name we call it, faith is a source of strength and a barrier against doubt. That's good enough for me.

FAITH

"Love is the only thing we can carry with us when we go, and it makes the end so easy."

—*LOUISA MAY ALCOTT*

"Faith is the seamstress
who mends our torn belief,
who sews the hems of childhood trust
and clips the threads of grief."

—*JOAN WALSH ANGLUND*

"I pray every single second of my life. Not on my knees—but with my work."

—*SUSAN B. ANTHONY*

"Love involves a peculiar unfathomable combination of understanding and misunderstanding."

—*DIANE ARBUS*

"The spirit of man is an inward flame, a lamp the world blows upon but never puts out."

—*MARGOT ASQUITH*

"Every act in consequence of our faith strengthens faith."

—*ANNA LETITIA BARBAULD*

"And not to forget that when life knocks you to your knees—well, that's the best position in which to pray, isn't it? On your knees. That's where I learned."

—*ETHEL BARRYMORE*

"Refusal to believe until proof is given is a rational position; denial of all outside of our own limited experience is absurd."

—*ANNIE BESANT*

"When I stand before God at the end of my life, I would hope that I would not have a single bit of talent left and could say: 'I used everything you gave me.'"

—*ERMA BOMBECK*

"All good fortune is a gift of the gods, and you don't win the favor of the ancient gods by being good, but by being bold."

—*ANITA BROOKNER*

"It is better to learn early of the inevitable depths, for then sorrow and death take their proper place in life, and one is not afraid."

—*PEARL S. BUCK*

"Thoughts—just mere thoughts—are as powerful as electric batteries—as good for one as sunlight is, or as bad for one as poison."

—*FRANCES HODGSON BURNETT*

"If thou wish to reach the perfection of love, it befits thee to set thy life in order."

—*SAINT CATHERINE OF SIENA*

"Every human being has, like Socrates, an attendant spirit; and wise are they who obey its signals. If it does not always tell us what to do, it always cautions us what not to do."
—*LYDIA MARIA CHILD*

"'Hope' is the thing with feathers
That perches in the soul
And sings the tune without the words
And never stops at all."

—*EMILY DICKINSON*

"Because I could not stop for Death,
He kindly stopped for me,
The carriage held but just Ourselves,
And Immortality."

—*EMILY DICKINSON*

"Change the mind, and the quality changes. Destroy the belief and tranquility disappears."
—*MARY BAKER EDDY*

"From science and from the spiritual experience of millions, we are discovering our capacity for endless awakenings in a universe of endless surprises."
—*MARILYN FERGUSON*

"Eternity is not something that begins after you are dead. It is going on all the time. We are in it now."
—*CHARLOTTE PERKINS GILMAN*

"All we are asked to bear we can bear. That is a law of the spiritual life. The only hindrance to the working of this law, as of all benign laws, is fear."

—*ELIZABETH GOUDGE*

"'Tis the strangest thing in the world that people should quarrel about religion, since we undoubtedly all mean the same thing; all good minds in every religion aim at pleasing the Supreme Being; the means we take differ according to where we are born, and the prejudices we imbibe from education—a consideration which ought to inspire us with kindness and indulgence to each other."

—*JANET GRAHAM*

"We could never learn to be brave and patient if there were only joy in the world."

—*HELEN KELLER*

"Divinity is in its omniscience and omnipotence like a wheel, a circle, a whole, that can neither be understood, nor divided, nor begun nor ended. The marvels of God are not brought forth from one's self. Rather, it is more like a chord, a sound that is played. The tone does not come out of the chord itself, but rather, through the touch of the musician. I am, of course, the lyre and harp of God's kindness."

—*HILDEGARD OF BINGEN*

"Commerce unites; religion divides."

—*ALICE TISDALE HOBART*

"There's nothing like a newborn baby to renew your spirit and to buttress your resolve to make the world a better place."

—*VIRGINIA KELLEY*

"The very least you can do in your life is to figure out what you hope for. And the most you can do is live inside that hope."

—*BARBARA KINGSOLVER*

"Only with winter patience can we bring
The deep-desired, long-awaited spring."

—*ANNE MORROW LINDBERGH*

"Fear makes strangers of people who should be friends."

—*SHIRLEY MACLAINE*

"I never knew a mocker who was not mocked...a deceiver who was not deceived, or a proud person who was not humbled."

—*MARGUERITE OF NAVARRE*

"No one ever perfectly loved God who did not perfectly love some of His creatures in this world."

—*MARGUERITE OF NAVARRE*

"Often God shuts a door in our face, and then subsequently opens the door through which we need to go."

—*CATHERINE MARSHALL*

"Religion is 'twixt God and my own soul;
Neither saint, nor sage, can boundless thought control."
　　　　　　　　　—*JUDITH SARGENT MURRAY*

"No one can arrive from being talented alone. God gives talent; work transforms talent into genius."
　　　　　　　　　—*ANNA PAVLOVA*

"All outward forms of religion are almost useless, and are the cause of endless strife. Believe there is a great power silently working all things for good, behave yourself and never mind the rest."
　　　　　　　　　—*BEATRIX POTTER*

"The future belongs to those who believe in the beauty of their dreams."
　　　　　　　　　—*ELEANOR ROOSEVELT*

"Spiritual power can be seen in a person's reverence for life—hers and all others, including animals and nature, with a recognition of a universal life force referred to by many as God."
　　　　　　　　　—*VIRGINIA SATIR*

"I realized a long time ago that a belief which does not spring from a conviction in the emotions is no belief at all."
　　　　　　　　　—*EVELYN SCOTT*

"One needs something to believe in, something for which one can have wholehearted enthusiasm."
　　　　　　　　　—*HANNAH SENESH*

"There is no religion without love, and people may talk as much as they like about their religion, but if it does not teach them to be good and kind to man and beast, it is all a sham."

—*ANNA SEWELL*

"Put your ear down close to your soul and listen hard."

—*ANNE SEXTON*

"Intuition is a spiritual faculty and does not explain, but simply points the way."

—*FLORENCE SCOVEL SHINN*

"To believe in something not yet proved and to underwrite it with our lives: it is the only way we can keep the future open. Man, surrounded by facts, permitting himself no surprise, no intuitive flash, no great hypothesis, no risk, is in a locked cell. Ignorance cannot seal the mind and imagination more securely."

—*LILLIAN SMITH*

"The fact that God has prohibited despair gives misfortune the right to hope all things, and leaves hope free to dare all things."

—*ANNE-SOPHIE SWETCHINE*

"It is strange how often a heart must be broken before the years can make it wise."

—*SARA TEASDALE*

"We must free ourselves to be filled by God. Even God cannot fill what is full."

—*MOTHER TERESA*

"Patience attains all that it strives for. He who has God finds he lacks nothing: God alone suffices."

— *SAINT TERESA OF AVILA*

"God knows no distance."

—*CHARLESZETTA WADDLES*

"With every deed you are sowing a seed, though the harvest you may not see."

—*ELLA WHEELER WILCOX*

5

FAMILY

*"No matter how many communes anybody invents,
the family always creeps back."*
—MARGARET MEAD

In my estimation, no compilation such as this book is complete
without quotations about *family*. What to some might seem a
rather restricted, or restrictive, category is, to me, one of the
most expansive.

Perhaps it depends upon how you define *family*. I see it,
and use it in this chapter, in its most encompassing sense: the
family of man, the family of nations, the family of belief, the
family of occupations, the family of friends and loved ones,
and, of course, the family that comprises each of our own
unique roots and heritage.

I see all of these various families as transmitting a sense of
identity, of belonging, of kinship. Family celebrates diversity as
well as commonality. Family implies a support base as well as a
multifaceted prism of identities.

For some given period of time in any given life, a work-
group or a class or a social or religious organization is a family of
sorts. If you're a speaker, an audience may be your family. And in
all of these cases, you may have the unique opportunity to help
a disparate group of individuals work, or at least think, together
to fulfill some set of common goals or desires.

Embracing the concept of family in its broadest sense is, I believe, an antidote to one of the greatest causes of organizational failure today—that sense of unconnectedness, of detachment, of aloneness and anonymity, perhaps most broadly defined as "alienation." But however you characterize it, it is symptomatic of a widespread societal need for belonging.

A shared concept of family, if only for a single project or activity, can be a powerful motivator for the restoration of individual spirits and can weld together a group that has little else in common. Some of the quotations in this chapter are intended to elaborate upon this holistic concept of family.

As unlikely as it may seem, I consider quotations about family to be, in their own way, as empowering to the reader, speaker, or listener as quotations about success, or character, or leadership.

I encourage the reader to seek out and develop her own collection of quotations that will enable her to communicate her own concepts and sense of family. They will be as empowering to her as the transmission of these quotations has been to me.

FAMILY

"Marriage is traditionally the destiny offered to women by society. Most women are married or have been, or plan to be or suffer from not being."

—*Simone de Beauvoir*

"A mother starts out as the most important person in her child's world and if she's successful in her work, she will eventually become the stupidest."

—*Mary Kay Blakely*

"Thanks to modern science women are able to have babies later and later. But waiting to give birth until it is covered by Medicare isn't going to fly. It's too risky for us to put a baby down and not remember where we left it."

—*Erma Bombeck*

"Never fear spoiling children by making them too happy. Happiness is the atmosphere in which all good affections grow."

—*Ann Eliza Bray*

"Anger repressed can poison a relationship as surely as the cruelest words."

—*Dr. Joyce Brothers*

"Our children are not treated with sufficient respect as human beings, and yet from the moment they are born they have this right to respect. We keep them children far too long, their world separate from the real world of life."
—*PEARL S. BUCK*

"Parents are their child's first teachers. As busy as they are, it's important to make time for their children."
—*LAURA BUSH*

"Climbing to the top of any profession takes a single-minded devotion that simply doesn't jibe well with being a parent."
—*LINDA CHAVEZ*

"It is not enough to preach about family values: we must value families."
—*HILLARY RODHAM CLINTON*

"When you educate a man you educate an individual; when you educate a woman you educate a whole family."
—*JOHNETTA B. COLE*

"My friends are my estate."
—*EMILY DICKINSON*

"I know there is strength in the differences between us. I know there is comfort where we overlap."
—*ANI DIFRANCO*

"Animals are such agreeable friends—they ask no questions, they pass no criticisms."
—*GEORGE ELIOT (MARY ANN EVANS)*

"I like not only to be loved, but to be told that I am loved; the realm of silence is large enough beyond the grave."
—*GEORGE ELIOT (MARY ANN EVANS)*

"A mother is not a person to lean on, but a person to make leaning unnecessary."
—*DOROTHY CANFIELD FISHER*

"Loving, like prayer, is a power as well as a process. It's curative. It is creative."
—*ZONA GALE*

"I knew it was normal and right in general, and held that a woman should be able to have marriage and motherhood, and do her work in the world, also."
—*CHARLOTTE PERKINS GILMAN*

"Fighting is essentially a masculine idea; a woman's weapon is her tongue."
—*HERMIONE GINGOLD*

"If you can't hold children in your arms, please hold them in your heart."
—*CLARA MCBRIDE HALE*

"Call it a clan, call it a network, call it a tribe, call it a family. Whatever you call it, whoever you are, you need one."
—*JANE HOWARD*

"I looked on child rearing not only as a work of love and duty but as a profession that was fully as interesting and challenging as any honorable profession in the world."
—*ROSE FITZGERALD KENNEDY*

"After a personal loss you realize a bullet is not the only thing that can pierce the heart."

—*LOU KERR*

"What its children become, that will the community become."

—*SUZANNE LAFOLLETTE*

"In the end, it's not what you do for your children but what you've taught them to do for themselves."

—*ANN LANDERS*

"In the small circle of the home woman has never quite forgotten the particular uniqueness of each member of the family; the spontaneity of now; the vividness of here. This is the basic substance of life. We find again some of the joy in the now, some of the peace in the here, some of the love in me and thee which go to make up the kingdom of heaven on earth."

—*ANNE MORROW LINDBERGH*

"When you are a mother you are never really alone in your thoughts. A mother always has to think twice, once for herself and once for her child."

—*SOPHIA LOREN*

"Ours is a circle of friendships united by ideals."

—*JULIETTE GORDON LOW*

"Woman knows what man has long forgotten: that the ultimate economic and spiritual unit of any civilization is still the family."

—*CLARE BOOTHE LUCE*

"We don't accomplish anything in this world alone, and whatever happens is the result of the whole tapestry of one's life and all the weavings of individual threads from one to another that creates something."

—*SANDRA DAY O'CONNOR*

"The best way to keep children at home is to make the home atmosphere pleasant and to let the air out of the tires."

—*DOROTHY PARKER*

"Kids learn more from example than anything you say. I'm convinced they learn very early not to hear anything you say, but watch what you do."

—*JANE PAULEY*

"Don't bring your worries to the playground. Work can be an insatiable beast. There is never enough time. You have to determine your parameters. That's why I'm eager for more women in high-level positions, because they understand the importance of balance."

—*NANCY PELOSI*

"Like all parents, my husband and I just do the best we can, hold our breath and hope we've set aside enough money for our kid's therapy."

—*MICHELLE PFEIFFER*

"Home is any four walls that enclose the right person."

—*HELEN ROWLAND*

"My husband and I are either going to buy a dog or have a child. We can't decide whether to ruin our carpet or ruin our lives."

—*RITA RUDNER*

"Families are ecosystems. Each life grows in response to the lives around it."

—*MARY SCHMICH*

"Prejudice? I experienced some, but it never hurts you so much as it hurts when your child experiences it."

—*ANNA MOORE SHAW*

"War is not the normal state of the human family in its higher development, but merely a feature of barbarism lasting on through the transition of the race, from the savage to the scholar."

—*ELIZABETH CADY STANTON*

"Absence is one of the most useful ingredients of family life, and to dose it rightly is an art like any other."

—*FREYA STARK*

"What can you do to promote world peace? Go home and love your family."

—*MOTHER TERESA*

"Every woman and every man, too, must take responsibility in their hearts for all children. As the parental generation, every child is our child. To ignore the state of our children is to ignore the state of our world."

—*MARIANNE WILLIAMSON*

"Mothers are really the true spiritual leaders."

—*OPRAH WINFREY*

6

HUMOR

"Life can be wildly tragic at times, and I've had my share. But whatever happens to you, you have to keep a lightly comic attitude. In the final analysis, you have got not to forget to laugh."
—KATHARINE HEPBURN

I can't imagine anything worse than being around people with no sense of *humor*. And I can't imagine anything more healthy than a hearty laugh.

I personally subscribe to the theory that laughter is genuinely, physiologically therapeutic. When you laugh, when you cause others to laugh, not only do you bring people together in a shared moment of joy, you are also helping people increase the flow of oxygen to their brains. So humor enriches both the mind and the body. And I truly believe that it does.

Selecting a compilation of quotations about humor was itself laugh-generating. My basic rule was that if a quotation didn't cause me to laugh out loud, chuckle, or at least smile, then I didn't include it.

My deal-killer on selecting these quotations was the line between the use of humor and the telling of a joke. Whether in a speech, a presentation, or in conversation, I seldom tell a joke. But I love to include bits of humor, especially self-deprecating humor. I learned many years ago that the ability to laugh at yourself is one of the most empowering things you can do. It makes you human, it allows people to get a tiny peek into who you really are, and it is one of the most disarming actions you can take.

I also included this chapter of quotations because I want to encourage women to lighten up a bit, learn to laugh at and with themselves, and use humor as a basically humanizing act.

I think women have for so many years either been relegated to the sidelines of, for example, the business world, or else have felt that in order to move off the sidelines and into the game they had to dress like men, talk like men, be "tough" like men, and think like men in order to compete with men. This process, I fear, had the effect of diminishing the very qualities of humanity and sensitivity that are the hallmark of so many successful women, once they allow those traits to emerge. Another trait that is perhaps just as important is to have a sense of humor. I have found that it is very hard to argue with someone with whom I have just shared a good laugh!

HUMOR

"He should go to a spa and lose some ego."

—*Bella Abzug*

"Time wounds all heels."

—*Jane Sherwood Ace*

"Most plain girls are virtuous because of the scarcity of opportunity to be otherwise."

—*Maya Angelou*

"I married beneath me; all women do."

—*Lady Nancy Astor*

"It is always incomprehensible to a man that a woman should refuse an offer of marriage."

—*Jane Austen*

"One cannot be always laughing at a man without now and then stumbling on something witty."

—*Jane Austen*

"The secret of staying young is to live honestly, eat slowly, and lie about your age."

—*Lucille Ball*

"I refuse to think of them as chin hairs. I think of them as stray eyebrows."

—*JANETTE BARBER*

"My husband said he needed more space. So I locked him outside."

—*ROSEANNE BARR*

"Every woman should marry twice. The first time for money, the second time for love."

—*ALVA BELMONT*

"I would love for my children to do something artistic. At the moment, they seem more interested in destruction than creativity."

—*CATE BLANCHETT*

"Love-matches are made by people who are content, for a month of honey, to condemn themselves to a life of vinegar."

—*LADY BLESSINGTON (MARGUERITE POWER GARDINER)*

"Next to hot chicken soup, a tattoo of an anchor on your chest, and penicillin, I consider a honeymoon one of the most overrated events in the world."

—*ERMA BOMBECK*

"I never liked the men I loved, and I never loved the men I liked."

—*FANNY BRICE*

"Truth-tellers are not always palatable. There is a preference for candy bars."

—*GWENDOLYN BROOKS*

"If the world were a logical place, men would ride side-saddle."

—*RITA MAE BROWN*

"Chocolate is the greatest gift to women ever created, next to the likes of Paul Newman and Gene Kelly. It's something that should be had on a daily basis."

—*SANDRA BULLOCK*

"There is nothing in the world like making people laugh."

—*CAROL BURNETT*

"Love is so much better when you are not married."

—*MARIA CALLAS*

"It doesn't matter what you do in the bedroom as long as you don't do it in the street and frighten the horses."

—*MRS. PATRICK CAMPBELL (BEATRICE STELLA TANNER)*

"As long as you know most men are like children, you know something."

—*COCO CHANEL*

"The trouble with some women is that they get all excited about nothing—and then marry him."

—*CHER*

"An archaeologist is the best husband a woman can have. The older she gets, the more interested he is in her."
—*AGATHA CHRISTIE*

"One keeps forgetting old age up to the very brink of the grave."
—*COLETTE*

"Total absence of humor renders life impossible."
—*COLETTE*

"Wisdom comes with age—if we can remember what we were talking about."
—*BETTE DAVIS*

"I should never have married, but I didn't want to live without a man. Brought up to respect the conventions, love had to end in marriage. I'm afraid it did."
—*BETTE DAVIS*

"In the beginning there was nothing. God said, 'Let there be light!' And there was light. There was still nothing but you could see it a whole lot better."
—*ELLEN DEGENERES*

"Careful grooming may take twenty years off a woman's age, but you can't fool a long flight of stairs."
—*MARLENE DIETRICH*

"They say it is better to be poor and happy than rich and miserable, but how about a compromise like moderately rich and just moody?"

—*Princess Diana*

"You've got to realize when all goes well, and everything is beautiful, you have no comedy. It's when somebody steps on the bride's train or belches during the ceremony, then you've got comedy."

—*Phyllis Diller*

"The major concrete achievement of the women's movement of the 1970s was the Dutch treat."

—*Nora Ephron*

"The reason the All-American boy prefers beauty to brains is that he can see better than he can think."

—*Farrah Fawcett*

"A man in love is incomplete until he is married. Then he's finished."

—*Zsa Zsa Gabor*

"Getting divorced just because you don't love a man is almost as silly as getting married just because you do."

—*Zsa Zsa Gabor*

"Whatever wrinkles I got, I enjoyed getting them."

—*Ava Gardner*

"If love means never having to say you're sorry, then marriage means always having to say everything twice. Husbands, due to an unknown quirk of the universe, never hear you the first time."

—*ESTELLE GETTY*

"It all goes back, of course, to Adam and Eve—a story which shows among other things, that if you make a woman out of a man, you are bound to get into trouble."

—*CAROL GILLIGAN*

"Dreams can come true. Now, whether they last—that's another thing."

—*WHOOPI GOLDBERG*

"If high heels were so wonderful, men would still be wearing them."

—*SUE GRAFTON*

"Mothers, food, love, and career; the four major guilt groups."

—*CATHY GUISEWITE*

"Whenever I dwell for any length of time on my own shortcomings, they gradually begin to seem mild, harmless, rather engaging little things, not at all like the staring defects in other people's character."

—*MARGARET HALSEY*

"Money is what you'd get on beautifully without if only other people weren't so crazy about it."

—*MARGARET CASE HARRIMAN*

"I would rather have bad things written about me than be forgotten."

—*PAMELA HARRIMAN*

"Inside me lives a skinny woman crying to get out. But I can usually shut her up with cookies."

—*HELEN HAYES*

"It is the plain women who know about love; the beautiful women are too busy being fascinating."

—*KATHARINE HEPBURN*

"The success or failure of a life, as far as posterity goes, seems to lie in the more or less luck of seizing the right moment of escape."

—*ALICE JAMES*

"Sainthood is acceptable only in saints."

—*PAMELA HANSFORD JOHNSON*

"Beware of the man who praises women's liberation. He is about to quit his job."

—*ERICA JONG*

"You see a lot of smart guys with dumb women, but you hardly ever see a smart woman with a dumb guy."

—*ERICA JONG*

"If men could become pregnant, abortion would be a sacrament."

—*FLORYNCE KENNEDY*

"Being divorced is like being hit by a Mack truck. If you live through it, you start looking very carefully to the right and to the left."

—*JEAN KERR*

"Few people know clearly what they want. Most people can't even think what to hope for when they throw a penny in a fountain."

—*BARBARA KINGSOLVER*

"I don't see much of Alfred any more since he got so interested in sex."

—*CLARE (MRS. ALFRED) KINSEY*

"A gossip is one who talks to you about others, a bore is one who talks to you about himself, and a brilliant conversationalist is one who talks to you about yourself."

—*LISA KIRK*

"You can safely assume that you've created God in your own image when it turns out that God hates all the same people you do."

—*ANNE LAMOTT*

"Don't accept your dog's admiration as conclusive evidence that you are wonderful."

—*ANN LANDERS*

"Nobody says you must laugh, but a sense of humor can help you overlook the unattractive, tolerate the unpleasant, cope with the unexpected, and smile through the day."

—*ANN LANDERS*

"I am not the type that wants to go back to the land; I am the type who wants to go back to the hotel."

—*FRAN LEBOWITZ*

"God is love, but get it in writing."

—*GYPSY ROSE LEE*

"When action grows unprofitable, gather information; when information grows unprofitable, sleep."

—*URSULA K. LEGUIN*

"A good laugh heals a lot of hurts."

—*MADELEINE L'ENGLE*

"Laughter by definition is healthy."

—*DORIS LESSING*

"I have a simple philosophy. Fill what is empty. Empty what's full. And scratch what itches."

—*ALICE ROOSEVELT LONGWORTH*

"Fun is fun but no girl wants to laugh all of the time."
—*ANITA LOOS*

"Kissing your hand may make you feel very good but a diamond and sapphire bracelet lasts forever."
—*ANITA LOOS*

"It is ridiculous to think that you can spend your entire life with just one person. Three is about the right number. Yes, I imagine three husbands would do it."
—*CLARE BOOTHE LUCE*

"Life is a combination of comedy and tragedy. Some of the funniest things I've ever heard were said at funerals."
—*SHIRLEY MACLAINE*

"To be wildly enthusiastic or deadly serious—both are wrong. Both pass. One must keep ever present a sense of humor."
—*KATHERINE MANSFIELD*

"The only truly safe and proper subject for a joke is oneself. Many a person who thought this privilege extended to his or her spouse, parent, or child has lived—but not very long— to find out otherwise."
—*JUDITH MARTIN ("MISS MANNERS")*

"Laugh at yourself first, before anybody else can."
—*ELSA MAXWELL*

"You mustn't force sex to do the work of love or love to do the work of sex."

—*MARY MCCARTHY*

"Women want mediocre men and men are working hard to be as mediocre as possible."

—*MARGARET MEAD*

"My idea of a superwoman is someone who scrubs her own floor."

—*BETTE MIDLER*

"Surely a king who loves pleasure is less dangerous than one who loves glory."

—*NANCY MITFORD*

"I've been on a calendar, but I've never been on time."

—*MARILYN MONROE*

"Cosmetics is a boon to every woman, but a girl's best beauty aid is still a near-sighted man."

—*YOKO ONO*

"By the time you swear you're his,
Shivering and sighing,
And he vows his passion is
Infinite, undying—
Lady, make a note of this:
One of you is lying."

—*DOROTHY PARKER*

"I require only three things of a man. He must be handsome, ruthless, and stupid."

—*DOROTHY PARKER*

"I'm not offended by all the dumb blonde jokes because I know I'm not dumb. I'm also not blonde."

—*DOLLY PARTON*

"Laughter is God's hand on a troubled world."
—*MINNIE PEARL (SARAH OPHELIA COLLEY CANNON)*

"A man hasn't got a corner on virtue just because his shoes are shined."

—*ANN PETRY*

"A complete revolution takes place in your physical and mental being when you've laughed and had some fun."
—*CATHERINE PONDER*

"Let me tell you, sisters, seeing dried egg on a plate in the morning is a lot dirtier than anything I've had to deal with in politics."

—*ANN RICHARDS*

"I once had a rose named after me and I was very flattered. But I was not pleased to read the description in the catalogue: 'No good in a bed, but fine up against a wall.'"
—*ELEANOR ROOSEVELT*

"In olden times sacrifices were made at the altar—a practice which is still continued."

—*HELEN ROWLAND*

"When you see what some girls marry, you realize how they must hate to work for a living."

—*HELEN ROWLAND*

"If you never want to see a man again say, 'I love you. I want to marry you. I want to have children.' They leave skid marks."

—*RITA RUDNER*

"Whenever I date a guy, I think, is this the man I want my children to spend their weekends with?"

—*RITA RUDNER*

"I like men to behave like men—strong and childish."

—*FRANÇOISE SAGAN*

"Friendship is like putting on a pair of pantyhose. You have to get one foot in and then the other, and wiggle around and tug until you get it right."

—*SUSAN SAINT JAMES*

"Women dress alike all over the world: they dress to be annoying to other women."

—*ELSA SCHIAPARELLI*

"I find intellectuals are more interested in gossip than anybody else."

—*DOROTHY SCHIFF*

"Woman's virtue is man's greatest invention."

—*CORNELIA OTIS SKINNER*

"A successful woman preacher was once asked, 'What special obstacles have you met as a woman in the ministry?' 'Not one,' she answered, 'except the lack of a minister's wife.'"

—*ANNA GARLIN SPENCER*

"The more I see of men, the more I like dogs."

—*MADAME DE STAËL*

"In America everybody is, but some are more than others."

—*GERTRUDE STEIN*

"Someone once asked me why women don't gamble as much as men do, and I gave the commonsensical reply that we don't have as much money. That is a true but incomplete answer. In fact, women's total instinct for gambling is satisfied by marriage."

—*GLORIA STEINEM*

"I think every woman is entitled to a middle husband she can forget."

—*ADELA ROGERS ST. JOHNS*

"Standing in the middle of the road is very dangerous; you get knocked down by the traffic from both sides."
—*MARGARET THATCHER*

"If love is the answer, could you rephrase the question?"
—*LILY TOMLIN*

"Instead of working for the survival of the fittest, we should be working for the survival of the wittiest; then we can all die laughing."
—*LILY TOMLIN*

"From birth to age 18 a girl needs good parents. From 18 to 35 she needs good looks. From 35 to 55 she needs a good personality. From 55 on she needs good cash."
—*SOPHIE TUCKER*

"Ever consider what pets must think of us? I mean, here we come back from a grocery store with the most amazing haul —chicken, pork, half a cow. They must think we're the greatest hunters on earth!"
—*ANNE TYLER*

"Age is a matter of mind—If you don't mind, it doesn't matter."
—*CAROLYN WARNER*

"I generally resist temptation unless I can't resist it."
—*MAE WEST*

"It's not the men in my life that count—it's the life in my men."

—*MAE WEST*

"Fools rush in—and get all the best seats."

—*MARYBETH WESTON*

"Whatever women must do they must do twice as well as men to be thought half as good. Luckily, this is not difficult."

—*CHARLOTTE WHITTON*

"Charm is the ability to make someone else think that both of you are pretty wonderful."

—*KATHLEEN WINSOR*

"I have lost friends, some by death...others by sheer inability to cross the street."

—*VIRGINIA WOOLF*

7

LEADERSHIP

*"A nation's strength ultimately consists in what it can do
on its own, and not in what it can borrow from others."*
—INDIRA GANDHI

There is no such thing as a one-size-fits-all template for *leader-ship*, any more than there is such a thing as the prototypical leader—male or female. Leaders come in all shapes and sizes, of all ages, from all corners of this nation and the globe, and with many different motivations, challenges, and opportunities. But they all have one thing in common: they are superb communicators, as well as being innate teachers and willing learners.

The Japanese word for teacher is *sensei*, which means far more than just someone who instructs. The literal meaning of the word is *honored leader*. A *sensei* is a guide, a mentor, a giver and sharer not just of information, but of knowledge. And when I think of the greatest leaders that I know, or have studied, they combine all of these qualities.

When it comes to women as leaders, I have frequently run up against the reality that far too many women simply don't think of themselves as having the capacity, the natural instincts, to be a leader.

Setting aside the historical reality that women have always been the cohesive force that held the family together, the basic flaw in that perception is this: leadership is not a genetic trait.

And, while leadership may be an inexact science, difficult to quantify in many respects, it is not an inert science. It is also not a theoretical science; it is an applied science, because its component qualities—planning, organization, commitment, effort, and action, to name but five—can all be taught, practiced, learned, and ingrained into one's personal way of living, thinking, and doing. You can't teach speed, and you can't learn to be tall, but you can most assuredly learn to be a leader.

Thus, I have chosen a compilation of quotations on leadership by women who have, each in her own way, learned and utilized leadership skills. The only challenge has been in finding as many quotations by women on this subject as I would like. I attribute this to the reality that, for so many years, the woman leader was the exception in the world in which she lived. But as more women take their places among the foremost leaders in our contemporary world, and as more young women have prior generations of such women to use as examples, I am confident that each succeeding edition of this book will offer a wider and more powerful selection than ever before of significant quotations by women leaders.

LEADERSHIP

"I've learned that people will forget what you said, people will forget what you did, but people will never forget how you made them feel."

—*Maya Angelou*

"No cause is left but the most ancient of all, the one, in fact, that from the beginning of our history has determined the very existence of politics: the cause of freedom versus tyranny."

—*Hannah Arendt*

"Power and violence are opposites; where the one rules absolutely, the other is absent."

—*Hannah Arendt*

"The time when you need to do something is when no one else is willing to do it, when people are saying it can't be done."

—*Mary Frances Berry*

"We believe that any transformation of the world begins with the transformation of the self. For eventually, it is love, goodwill and cooperation which will overcome the negative forces threatening us and bring about the dawn of a new age. It is really the self to which we should aim to direct our efforts to rebuild. It is in a society that can inspire and foster individual drives that humans can prosper."

—*H.R.H. Basma Bint Talal*

"There is a rule in sailing where the more maneuverable ship should give way to the less maneuverable craft. I think this is sometimes a good rule to follow in human relations as well."
—DR. *JOYCE BROTHERS*

"People on the whole are very simple-minded, in whatever country one finds them. They are so simple as to take literally, more often than not, the things their leaders tell them."
—*PEARL S. BUCK*

"Let's all be brothers for this better world, giving a hand to the ones who do not have, telling them: come with me, I will help you; we will fill their eyes with light and this better world will bring them the gift of the smile of life."
—*MONTSERRAT CABALLÉ*

"When a just cause reaches its flood tide, whatever stands in the way must fall before its overwhelming power."
—*CARRIE CHAPMAN CATT*

"We need leaders once again who can tap into that special blend of American confidence and optimism that has enabled generations before us to meet our toughest challenges. Leaders who can help us show ourselves and the world that with our ingenuity, creativity, and innovative spirit, there are no limits to what is possible in America."
—*HILLARY RODHAM CLINTON*

"I think I'm a better leader in my job because I'm a parent. I'm a lower-stress person, more organized and have learned how to set priorities because of my children."

—*EILEEN COLLINS*

"Democracy doesn't recognize east or west; democracy is simply people's will. Therefore, I do not acknowledge that there are various models of democracy; there is just democracy itself."

—*SHIRIN EBADI*

"I cannot lead you into battle. I do not give you laws or administer justice, but I can do something else—I can give my heart and my devotion to these old islands and to all the peoples of our brotherhood of nations."

—*QUEEN ELIZABETH II*

"I offer the voters experience, not an experiment."

—*ANA FROHMILLER*

"Have a bias toward action—let's see something happen now. You can break that big plan into small steps and take the first step right away."

—*INDIRA GANDHI*

"Power in itself has never attracted me, nor has position been my goal. My resolve will in fact be all the more firm, to fight for our principles, for our vision, and for our ideals."

—*SONIA GANDHI*

"The hardest times for me were not when people challenged what I said, but when I felt my voice was not heard."
—*CAROL GILLIGAN*

"After all, that is what laws are for, to be made and unmade."
—*EMMA GOLDMAN*

"If a law commands me to sin I will break it; if it calls me to suffer, I will let it take its course unresistingly. The doctrine of the blind obedience and unqualified submission to any human power, whether civil or ecclesiastical, is the doctrine of despotism, and ought to have no place."
—*ANGELINA GRIMKE*

"Crisis is an opportunity. It cannot be avoided so take advantage of it. We must seize this unique opportunity to reshape the world to meet the challenges of the 21st century."
—*DALIA GRYBAUSKAITE*

"It must be possible in a democracy to devote sufficient resources to the protection of minorities and their rights."
—*DALIA GRYBAUSKAITE*

"I see something that has to be done and I organize it."
—*ELINOR GUGGENHEIMER*

"It requires courage and vision to take the lead when hope and commitment to the whole agenda are on the wane."
—*SARAH HARDER*

"Leadership is a communal responsibility with a concern for the welfare of the people or tribe and then sharing the work that needs to be done based on skills and abilities. Leadership is shared responsibility and promoting people's well-being."
—*LaDonna Harris*

"The only way to make sure people you agree with can speak is to support the rights of people you don't agree with."
—*Eleanor Holmes Norton*

"Walk the street with us into history. Get off the sidewalk."
—*Dolores Huerta*

"I strongly believe that, in order to find solutions to our current problems, young people must be included in the equation. Because young people are not willing to merely follow in our footsteps. They are, in fact, usually one step ahead of us. They are the ones pulling us forward."
—*Michaelle Jean*

"The turtle is the sign of the risk taker: you can only make progress when you are willing to stick your neck out and put your tail on the line."
—*Dr. Effie Hall Jones*

"And now we must look to the future. Let us heed the voice of the people and recognize their common sense. If we do not, we not only blaspheme our political heritage, we ignore the common ties that bind all Americans."
—*Barbara Jordan*

"We, the People. It is a very eloquent beginning. But when that document was completed on the seventeenth of September in 1787 I was not included in that 'We, the people.' I felt somehow for many years that George Washington and Alexander Hamilton just left me out by mistake. But through the process of amendment, interpretation and court decision, I have finally been included in 'We, the People.'"

—*BARBARA JORDAN*

"Though I am minister, I'm basically a scientist. That's right, I must be aware of my shortcomings and learn to be a qualified leader."

—*ZHU LILAN*

"Leaders are armed with genuine passion. Leaders understand the meaning of quiet sacrifice by putting others ahead of their own private interests. Leaders listen."

—*TAMI LONGABERGER*

"The work of today is the history of tomorrow, and we are its makers."

—*JULIETTE GORDON LOW*

"Women in leadership roles can help restore balance and wholeness to our communities."

—*WILMA MANKILLER*

"An unrectified case of injustice has a terrible way of lingering, restlessly, in the social atmosphere like an unfinished question."

—*MARY MCCARTHY*

"Humanity is still far from that stage of maturity needed for the realisation of its aspirations, for the construction, that is, of a harmonious and peaceful society and the elimination of wars. Men are not yet ready to shape their own destinies, to control and direct world events, of which—instead—they become victims."

—*MARIA MONTESSORI*

"Dare we believe that the leaders of the world's great nations will wake up, will see the precipice towards which they are moving, and change direction?"

—*ALVA MYRDAL*

"The misconception that 'a victory is worth the price' has in the nuclear age become a total illusion."

—*ALVA MYRDAL*

"One hopes that all of one's background affects your modus operandi. I'm a retired cowgirl. I tend to the practical."

—*SANDRA DAY O'CONNOR*

"Those men and women are fortunate who are born at a time when great struggle for human freedom is in progress."

—*EMMELINE PANKHURST*

"I never doubted that equal rights was the right direction. Most reforms, most problems, are complicated. But to me there is nothing complicated about ordinary equality."

—*ALICE PAUL*

"Lawyers are operators of the toll bridge which anyone in search of justice must pass."

—JANE BRYANT QUINN

"If you see someone in law enforcement or education, please thank them, because they will never get enough money to do what they need to do."

—ANN RICHARDS

"I want to work for a company that contributes to and is part of the community. I want something not just to invest in. I want something to believe in."

—ANITA RODDICK

"We have to face the fact that either all of us are going to die together or we are going to learn to live together, and if we are to live together we have to talk."

—ELEANOR ROOSEVELT

"The Pueblo people and the indigenous people of the Americas see time as round, not a linear string. Think of time as an ocean, always moving."

—LESLIE MARMON SILKO

"I really do believe I can accomplish a great deal with a big grin. I know some people find that disconcerting, but that doesn't matter."

—BEVERLY SILLS

"It had long since come to my attention that people of ac-complishment rarely sit back and let things happen to them. They went out and happen to things."

—*ELINOR SMITH*

"The aspiration to impartiality is just that—it's an aspira-tion because it denies the fact that we are by our experiences making different choices than others."

—*SONIA SOTOMAYOR*

"Scientific progress makes moral progress a necessity; for if man's power is increased, the checks that restrain him from abusing it must be strengthened."

—*MADAME DE STAËL*

"We deceive ourselves when we fancy that only weakness needs support. Strength needs it far more."

—*ANNE-SOPHIE SWETCHINE*

"In every crisis there is a message. Crises are nature's way of forcing change—breaking down old structures, shaking loose negative habits so that something new and better can take their place."

—*SUSAN L. TAYLOR*

"Lifting as they climb, onward and upward they go, strug-gling and striving and hoping that the buds and blossoms of their desires may burst into glorious fruition ere long."

—*MARY CHURCH TERRELL*

"The older you get the more you realize that gray isn't such a bad color. And in politics you work with it or you don't work at all."

—*AGNES SLIGH TURNBULL*

"Great events make me quiet and calm; it is only trifles that irritate my nerves."

—*QUEEN VICTORIA*

"People call me a feminist whenever I express sentiments that differentiate me from a doormat or a prostitute."

—*REBECCA WEST*

"There is no chance, no destiny, no fate, that can circumvent or hinder or control the firm resolve of a determined soul."

—*ELLA WHEELER WILCOX*

"I have not contended for Democrat, Republican, Protestant or Baptist for an agent. I have worked for freedom, I have labored to give my race a voice in the affairs of the nation."

—*SARAH WINNEMUCCA*

"Talent matters and intelligence matters. Passion and caring, imagination, fire and spirit matter. Those who possess these qualities in abundance should lead us into the global future."

—*PATRICIA WOERTZ*

8

POLITICS

*"The most common way people give up their power
is by thinking they don't have any."*
—*ALICE WALKER*

Life *is politics*. And it has nothing to do with seeking or holding, winning or losing elective office. Life is politics at its very root, quite literally, because the word is derived from the Greek words for citizen and citizenship. Since there can be no true citizenship in the absence of participation, politics means being a part of the world around you—*all* the world, *all* around you! And this status is characteristic of essentially everything we do or come into contact with in life.

Unless we are members of a cloistered monastic order of hermits, we live, work, and function in the midst of other people. In this milieu, we spend a greater part of every waking hour trying to communicate, convince, direct, manage, interact, or in some way or other "politic" with every person with whom we come into contact—including ourselves. So regardless of what you call yourself or what you think you do, you and all around you are, in reality, "politicians."

The one word I always associate with politics is *participation*. You really can't have one without the other. Because politics, in both its narrowest and broadest senses, requires the participation of other people.

We often speak of the United States of America as a "participatory democracy." So is life. Persuasion—of anybody about any thing—requires some level of participation, and persuasion is the ultimate political art.

The outstanding examples of women in this field are too great to confine to one chapter. Thus, their quotations are scattered throughout this book. But included in this particular chapter are the words of women that can serve as an example of practically every form of participatory citizenship—from elective office, to leading or managing a business or organization (or a family), to volunteerism of every kind.

The words in these pages can serve as illustrations of the worth of participation, of investing in a cause. Some are self-deprecating and some are tongue-in-cheek. Some are distillations of truth so salient that reading the words invokes the almost instant mental response of "yes!" Some are expressions of frustration that reveal just how difficult it is to be a participant, let alone a successful one.

Regardless of how politics is practiced, or to what degree of success it is done, all these words represent the persuasive powers and the participatory strength of women.

POLITICS

"If particular care is not paid to the ladies, we are determined to foment a rebellion, and will not hold ourselves bound by any laws in which we have no voice, no representation."

—*ABIGAIL ADAMS*

"Nothing could be worse than the fear that one had given up too soon, and left one unexpended effort that might have saved the world."

—*JANE ADDAMS*

"Cautious, careful people, always casting about to preserve their reputation and social standing, never can bring about reform."

—*SUSAN B. ANTHONY*

"Liberty is a great celestial Goddess, strong, beneficent, and austere, and she can never descend upon a nation by the shouting of crowds, nor by arguments of unbridled passion, nor by the hatred of class against class."

—*ANNIE BESANT*

"Nothing crushes freedom as substantially as a tank."

—*SHIRLEY TEMPLE BLACK*

"A passion for politics stems usually from an insatiable need, either for power, or for friendship and adulation, or a combination of both."

—*FAWN M. BRODIE*

"None who have always been free can understand the terrible fascinating power of the hope of freedom to those who are not free."

—*PEARL S. BUCK*

"This is a time in history when women's voices must be heard, or forever be silenced. It's not because we think better than men, but we think differently. It's not women against men, but women and men. It's not that the world would have been better if women had run it, but that the world will be better when we as women, who bring our own perspective, share in running it."

—*BETTY BUMPERS*

"True democracy will only happen when we rid the people of the mentality that war and violence present solutions to our problems. Whatever problem arises, it can be resolved democratically. War never brings the answer, it only presents new problems."

—*VIOLETA BARRIOS DE CHAMORRO*

"U.S. politics is a beautiful fraud that has been imposed on the people for years, whose practitioners exchange gilded promises for the most valuable thing their victims own, their vote."

—*SHIRLEY CHISHOLM*

"The challenge now is to practice politics as the art of making what appears to be impossible, possible."
—*HILLARY RODHAM CLINTON*

"Women share with men the need for personal success, even the taste of power; and no longer are we willing to satisfy those needs through the achievements of surrogates— whether husbands, children or merely role models."
—*ELIZABETH DOLE*

"An election is coming. Universal peace is declared, and the foxes have a sincere interest in prolonging the lives of the poultry."
—*GEORGE ELIOT (MARY ANN EVANS)*

"The curious fascination in this job is the illusion that either you are being useful or you could be—and that's so tempting."
—*MILLICENT FENWICK*

"Freedom is not worth fighting for if it means no more than license for everyone to get as much as he can for himself."
—*DOROTHY CANFIELD FISHER*

"True, the movement for women's rights has broken many old fetters, but it has also forged new ones."
—*EMMA GOLDMAN*

"Once a president gets to the White House, the only audience that is left that really matters is history."
—*DORIS KEARNS GOODWIN*

"In politics, you cannot allow yourself to lose sight of the long term, of the strategic, simply because everyday life gets in the way. If we don't learn now, we will learn the hard way later."

—*DALIA GRYBAUSKAITE*

"We must learn to see power as the fuel which makes the system work, the sap which generates growth in plants, the electricity which turned on rural America. It is creative human energy which we reflect and share with one another, in which we discover new and better ways of doing things. This kind of power is used not to impose but to inspire."

—*SARAH HARDER*

"Senator, I am one of them. You do not seem to understand who I am. I am a Black woman, the daughter of a dining-car worker. If my life has any meaning at all, it is that those who start out as outcasts can wind up as being part of the system."

—*PATRICIA ROBERTS HARRIS*

"Most politicians will not stick their necks out unless they sense grass-roots support. Neither you nor I should expect someone else to take our responsibility. If we remain passive, they will surely win."

—*KATHARINE HEPBURN*

"The clash of ideas is the sound of freedom."

—*LADY BIRD JOHNSON*

"A government is not legitimate merely because it exists."
                              —JEANE J. KIRKPATRICK

"No woman has ever so comforted the distressed—or so distressed the comfortable—as Eleanor Roosevelt."
                              —CLARE BOOTHE LUCE

"Bureaucracy, the rule of no one, has become the modern form of despotism."
                              —MARY MCCARTHY

"Today the real test of power is not the capacity to make war but the capacity to prevent it."
                              —ANNE O'HARE MCCORMICK

"Never doubt that a small group of thoughtful, committed citizens can change the world. Indeed, it is the only thing that ever has."
                              —MARGARET MEAD

"It's no accident many accuse me of conducting public affairs with my heart instead of my head. Well, what if I do? Those who don't know how to weep with their whole heart don't know how to laugh either."
                              —GOLDA MEIR

"An aristocracy in a republic is like a chicken whose head has been cut off: it may run about in a lively way, but in fact it is dead."
                              —NANCY MITFORD

"The best art is political and you ought to be able to make it unquestionably political and irrevocably beautiful at the same time."

—*TONI MORRISON*

"The function of freedom is to free somebody else."

—*TONI MORRISON*

"My vision of the future is of a world in which cultural differences are respected both within and between countries; where the worth and dignity of all human beings are acknowledged and placed at the center of all thought and action; where true appreciation of each other's cultures will eliminate the impulse to dominate others."

—*GLORIA NIKOI*

"The essence of a free life is being able to choose the style of living you prefer free from exclusion and without the compulsion of conformity or law."

—*ELEANOR HOLMES NORTON*

"Those who act or refuse to act, without regard to the effect their action will have on individual lives, have a secret weapon: they only deal with statistics, because statistics can protect you from painful realizations."

—*ANTONIA COELLO NOVELLO*

"We are here, not because we are lawbreakers; we are here in our efforts to become law-makers."

—*EMMELINE PANKHURST*

"I believe my work in the Democratic Party and in politics is a continuation of my work as a mom. When people ask me what are the three most important issues facing the Congress, I always say, the same thing: Our children, our children, our children. Their health, their education, their economic security including the pension security of their grandparents, the environment in which they live, and a world at peace in which they can flourish."

—NANCY PELOSI

"As a nation, we must show our greatness, not just our strength. America must be a light in the world, not just a missile."

—NANCY PELOSI

"We cannot silence the voices that we do not like hearing. We can, however, do everything in our power to make certain that other voices are heard."

—DEBORAH PROTHROW-STITH

"To know the law is to know how to make this world better through its proper application. And to practice law properly is to engage in public service of the highest order."

—ANNA QUINDLEN

"I want to stand by my country, but I cannot vote for war. I vote no."

—JEANNETTE RANKIN

"Democracy forever teases us with the contrast between its ideals and its realities, between its heroic possibilities and its sorry achievements."

—*AGNES REPPLIER*

"I've always said that in politics, your enemies can't hurt you, but your friends will kill you."

—*ANN RICHARDS*

"Certain rights can never be granted to the government, but must be kept in the hands of the people."

—*ELEANOR ROOSEVELT*

"Who ever walked behind anyone to freedom? If we can't go hand in hand, I don't want to go."

—*HAZEL SCOTT*

"Before you can become a statesman you first have to get elected, and to get elected you have to be a politician pledging support for what the voters want."

—*MARGARET CHASE SMITH*

"But when at last woman stands on an even platform with man, his acknowledged equal everywhere, with the same freedom to express herself in the religion and government of the country, then, and not until then, will he be able to legislate as wisely and generously for her as for himself."

—*ELIZABETH CADY STANTON*

"Like all disfranchised classes, they began by asking to have certain wrongs redressed, and not by asserting their own right to make laws for themselves."

—*ELIZABETH CADY STANTON*

"Our 'pathway' is straight to the ballot box, with no variableness nor shadow of turning. We demand suffrage for all the citizens of the Republic. I would not talk of Negroes or women, but of citizens."

—*ELIZABETH CADY STANTON*

"The quest for democracy is the struggle of a people to live whole, meaningful lives as free and equal members of the world community."

—*AUNG SAN SUU KYI*

"Defeat in itself was part and parcel of the great gambling game of politics. A man who could not accept it and try again was not of the stuff of which leaders are made."

—*AGNES SLIGH TURNBULL*

"One of the things being in politics has taught me is that men are not a reasoned or reasonable sex."

—*MARGARET THATCHER*

"When poor people feel they make a difference, they vote. There's no apathy; there's disappointment."

—*DOROTHY TILLMAN*

"There is a debt to the Negro people which America can never repay. At least then, they must make amends."

—*SOJOURNER TRUTH*

"Relatively speaking, passing the laws and rules and regulations is simple. It is the doing part that is difficult."

—*CAROLYN WARNER*

"One had better die fighting against injustice than die like a dog or rat in a trap."

—*IDA B. WELLS-BARNETT*

"If the abstract rights of man will bear discussion and explanation, those of woman, by a parity of reasoning, will not shrink from the same test, though a different opinion prevails in the country."

—*MARY WOLLSTONECRAFT*

"The price of running for the Senate today is spending more time than you'd like to spend asking people for more money than they'd like to give."

—*HARRIET WOODS*

9

SELF-IMAGE

"We don't see things as they are; we see them as we are."
—ANAÏS NIN

One of the most loaded words in our vocabulary is *ego*. It is almost a pejorative, which is unfortunate. There is absolutely nothing wrong with having a healthy ego, a positive *self-image*. After all, if you don't think well of yourself, who else will? Having an inner drive that helps to move you forward in life is not a sin; misusing it probably is. As with so many things, the essence and the excess tend to get confused.

One of the most powerful motivating forces in the world is a person's image of herself at her future best. That is what having a healthy self-image, a healthy ego, is all about. Self-image is the tool that either inhibits and holds us back, or activates and elevates us to be and do our best.

The biblical admonition to "Love thy neighbor as thyself" presents an interesting spin on the concept of self-image. Perhaps that maxim is the reason one should have a positive self-image, for how can you extend to another something that you yourself lack? Conversely, not loving yourself can quickly translate into views, attitudes, and expectations of others that are equally limited and negative. A poor self-image radiates outward like toxic smog onto all who come into contact with you just as surely as a positive one does. But the affect is considerably different.

I have chosen to include a chapter of quotations on self-image because I see them as encouraging and also cautionary notes to the women who read and, I hope, use them, whether in writing, presenting, or conversation.

These quotations by women and for women are especially important, I believe, because we women tend to be harder on ourselves than anybody else is ever likely to be. We often seem to work very hard to keep our self-image as subdued as possible. We aim for perfection and seldom forgive our inability to attain it. More than anything, I hope the words in this chapter help women focus less on being perfect and more on thinking well of themselves. You have to like yourself for your strengths and forgive yourself for your weaknesses—and do the same for others.

SELF-IMAGE

"If a woman just tries to stay toned and beautiful-looking on the outside but hasn't developed anything of value inside, there's not much to talk about."

—*DEBBIE ALLEN*

"My grandmother, who was one of the greatest human beings I've ever known, used to say, 'I am a child of God and I'm nobody's creature.' That to me defined the Black woman through the centuries."

—*MAYA ANGELOU*

"Each of us has the right and the responsibility to assess the roads which lie ahead and, if the future road looms ominous or unpromising, then we need to gather our resolve and step off, into another direction."

—*MAYA ANGELOU*

"Thoughts, rest your wings. Here is a hollow of silence, a nest of stillness, in which to hatch your dreams."

—*JOAN WALSH ANGLUND*

"You never find yourself until you tell the truth."

—*PEARL BAILEY*

"Long tresses down to the floor can be beautiful, if you have that, but learn to love what you have."

—*ANITA BAKER*

"I think knowing what you cannot do is more important than knowing what you can do. In fact, that's good taste."

—*LUCILLE BALL*

"My heart is as pure as the driven slush."

—*TALLULAH BANKHEAD*

"It is sad to grow old but nice to ripen."

—*BRIGITTE BARDOT*

"A woman is beautiful when she thinks she is."

—*ETHEL BARRYMORE*

"Pity is the deadliest feeling that can be offered to a woman."

—*VICKI BAUM*

"The armored cars of dreams contrived to let us do so many a dangerous thing."

—*ELIZABETH BISHOP*

"When I was fourteen, I was the oldest I ever was. I've been getting younger ever since."

—*SHIRLEY TEMPLE BLACK*

"It takes a lot of courage to show your dreams to someone else."

—*ERMA BOMBECK*

"Follow your dream. Take one step at a time and don't settle for less, just continue to climb."

—*AMANDA BRADLEY*

"Oh, grieve not, ladies, if at night,
Ye wake to feel your beauty going;
It was a web of frail delight,
Inconstant as an April snowing."

—*ANNA BRANCH*

"I've dreamt in my life dreams that have stayed with me ever after, and changed my ideas; they've gone through and through me, like wine through water, and altered the color of my mind."

—*EMILY BRONTË*

"No one can build [her] security upon the nobleness of another person."

—*WILLA CATHER*

"How many cares one loses when one decides not to be something, but someone."

—*COCO CHANEL*

"Relationships are like pressures that push you in 36 directions on the compass. But, as in a crowded streetcar, if you learn how to maintain your balance against all the weights, you might arrive at yourself."

—*DIANA CHANG*

"People are uncertain because they don't have the self-confidence to make decisions."

—*JULIA CHILD*

"I might have been born in a hovel, but I am determined to travel with the wind and the stars."

—*JACQUELINE COCHRAN*

"A person's best ally is someone who takes care of herself."

—*SUSAN CLARKE*

"I look in the mirror through the eyes of the child that was me."

—*JUDY COLLINS*

"Don't be afraid of the space between your dreams and reality. If you can dream it, you can make it so."

—*BELVA DAVIS*

"Beauty does not come with creams and lotions. God can give us beauty, but whether that beauty remains or changes is determined by our thoughts and deeds. A woman who leads a lazy life will reflect it in her face."

—*DELORES DEL RIO*

"Everyone needs to be valued. Everyone has the potential to give something back."

—*PRINCESS DIANA*

"We never know how high we are
Till we are called to rise;
And then, if we are true to plan,
Our statures touch the skies."

—*EMILY DICKINSON*

"A charm invests a face
Imperfectly beheld,
The lady dare not lift her veil
For fear it be dispelled."

—*EMILY DICKINSON*

"Spirit is the real and eternal; matter is the unreal and temporal."

—*MARY BAKER EDDY*

"There are two entirely opposite attitudes possible in facing the problems of one's life. One, to try and change the external world, the other, to try and change oneself."

—*JOANNA FIELD*

"You have to master not only the art of listening to your head, you must also master listening to your heart and listening to your gut."

—*CARLY FIORINA*

"It is very difficult to be two simple people at once, one who wants to have a law to itself and the other who wants to keep all the nice old things and be loved and safe and protected."

—*ZELDA FITZGERALD*

"Let us give up our favourite trait of being 'unendingly argumentative' and for a change let us be 'effectively collaborative.'"

—*SONIA GANDHI*

"When uncertainty about her own worth prevents a woman from claiming equality, self-assertion falls prey to the old criticism of selfishness."

—*CAROL GILLIGAN*

"The things we hate about ourselves aren't more real than the things we like about ourselves."

—*ELLEN GOODMAN*

"The thing that makes you exceptional is inevitably that which must also make you lonely."

—*LORRAINE HANSBERRY*

"Only you can determine your own worth, your own self-esteem and how much happiness to expect in life."

—*JINGER HEATH*

"If I don't have friends, then I ain't nothing."

—*BILLIE HOLIDAY*

"Surviving means being born over and over."

—*ERICA JONG*

"Birds sing after a storm; why shouldn't people feel as free to delight in whatever remains to them?"

—*ROSE FITZGERALD KENNEDY*

"Through the eyes of a child you can see your soul, feel your pain and know your happiness."

—*LOU KERR*

"Being solitary is being alone well: being alone luxuriously immersed in doing your own choice, aware of the fullness of your own presence rather than of the absence of others. Because solitude is an achievement."

—*ALICE KOLLER*

"The ultimate lesson all of us have to learn is unconditional love, which includes not only others but ourselves as well."
—*ELISABETH KÜBLER-ROSS*

"Perfectionism is the voice of the oppressor."
—*ANNE LAMOTT*

"We decided that it was no good asking what is the meaning of life, because life isn't an answer, life is the question, and you, yourself, are the answer."
—*URSULA K. LEGUIN*

"The great thing about getting older is that you don't lose all the other ages you've been."
—*MADELEINE L'ENGLE*

"Think wrongly, if you please, but in all cases think for yourself."
—*DORIS LESSING*

"I was afraid that if I didn't challenge myself, I wouldn't be true to who I really am. If I had listened to the fears, I never would have done half the things I've done."
—*JUDITH LIGHT*

"Happiness for the average person may be said to flow largely from common sense, adapting oneself to circumstances, and a sense of humor."
—*BEATRICE LILLIE*

"When one is a stranger to oneself, then one is estranged from others, too."

—ANNE MORROW LINDBERGH

"If I didn't define myself for myself, I would be crunched into other people's fantasies for me and eaten alive."

—AUDRE LORDE

"I don't need a man to validate my existence. The most profound relationship we'll ever have is the one with ourselves."

—SHIRLEY MACLAINE

"One of the things my parents taught me, and I'll always be grateful for the gift, is to not ever let anybody else define me."

—WILMA MANKILLER

"Risk! Risk anything! Care no more for the opinions of others, for those voices. Do the hardest thing on earth for you. Act for yourself. Face the truth."

—KATHERINE MANSFIELD

"One must be true to one's vision of life, in every single particular. The only thing to do is to try from tonight to be stronger and better—to be whole."

—KATHERINE MANSFIELD

"A woman of honor should not suspect another of things she would not do herself."

—QUEEN MARGARET (MARGUERITE DE VALOIS)

"Can't nothing make your life work if you ain't the architect."
—*TERRY MCMILLAN*

"Dreams are illustrations from the book your soul is writing about you."

—*MARSHA NORMAN*

"We can shield ourselves against personal knowledge of individual human misery if we concentrate only on the numbers, the science, the abstractions, the statistics. But at the end of the day, can we ever really escape from the knowledge that every number is a face without tears—that up close, every statistic is some mother's child?"

—*ANTONIA COELLO NOVELLO*

"We want our children and all children in this nation to know that the only limit to the height of your achievements is the reach of your dreams and your willingness to work."

—*MICHELLE OBAMA*

"I wake up with new dreams every day. And the more you do, when you're a dreamer, the more everything creates other arenas you can go into. It's like a tree with many branches, and branches with many leaves."

—*DOLLY PARTON*

"I have always made a distinction between my friends and my confidants. I enjoy the conversation of the former; from the latter I hide nothing."

—*Edith Piaf*

"She must learn to speak, starting with I, starting with We, starting as the infant does, with her own true hunger, and pleasure, and rage."

—*Marge Piercy*

"Five promises anchor our efforts to help young people succeed in life; they need caring adults, safe places (homes or schools), a healthy start, effective education, and opportunities to help others."

—*Alma Powell*

"The thing that is really hard, and really amazing, is giving up on being perfect and beginning the work of becoming yourself."

—*Anna Quindlen*

"Love is an expression and assertion of self-esteem, a response to one's own values in the person of another."

—*Ayn Rand*

"No one can make you feel inferior without your consent."

—*Eleanor Roosevelt*

"It is our choices that show what we truly are, far more than our abilities."

—*J. K. ROWLING*

"There is a proper balance between not asking enough of oneself and asking or expecting too much."

—*MAY SARTON*

"I feel as though I will always be a work in progress. And while I recognize my situation is unique, I am like the majority of women—trying to find a way to write my own legacy while balancing and respecting the other legacies I bear."

—*MARIA SHRIVER*

"This is what 40 looks like? We've been lying so long, who would know."

—*GLORIA STEINEM*

"To learn to know one's self, to pursue the avenues of self-development is what I call creative aging."

—*ADA BARNETT STOUGH*

"Whatever we believe about ourselves and our abilities comes true for us."

—*SUSAN L. TAYLOR*

"Challenges make you discover things about yourself that you never really knew. They're what make the instrument stretch—what makes you go beyond the norm."

—*CICELY TYSON*

"A woman who has no way of expressing herself and of realizing herself as a human being has nothing else to turn to but the owning of material things."

—*ENRIQUETA LONGEAUX Y VÁSQUEZ*

"To feel valued, to know even if only once in a while, that you can do a job well is an absolutely marvelous feeling."

—*BARBARA WALTERS*

"Through travel I first became aware of the outside world; it was through travel that I found my own introspective way into becoming a part of it."

—*EUDORA WELTY*

"One can remain alive long past the usual date of disintegration if one is unafraid of change, insatiable in intellectual curiosity, interested in big things and happy in small ways."

—*EDITH WHARTON*

"Kinder the enemy who must malign us
Than the smug friend who will define us."

—*ANNA WICKHAM*

"It doesn't happen all at once. You become. It takes a long time."

—MARGERY WILLIAMS

"You cannot move freely, speak freely, act freely, be free, unless you are comfortable with yourself."

—OPRAH WINFREY

"Love between two people is such a precious thing. It is not a possession. I no longer need to possess to complete myself. True love becomes my freedom."

—ANGELA L. WOZNIAK

10

SUCCESS

"We are not interested in the possibilities of defeat."
—QUEEN VICTORIA

Success can be many things: a fact, an attitude, or a sort of mental ambience. When presenting yourself to the world, it is best to try and radiate all three.

Being a success doesn't mean being a household word. It doesn't mean material wealth. It doesn't necessarily even mean being better than anybody else at what you do. But it *does* mean having the attitudinal comfort, the positive self-image, and the absolute certainty that comes with being as well-prepared as you can possibly be for any eventuality, any task. These are the combined qualities that will allow you to be and to do your very best. If you *are* those things, then you will be perceived that way, and you will *be* a success.

Success and self-image are very much kin to each other. I have seldom seen a woman with a positive and effective self-image who was not successful in most of her endeavors. I have, however, seen far too many women who were by any measure a success, but whose self-image gave no hint.

The quotations in this chapter about success approach it from every perspective: personal, organizational, and attitudinal. The women quoted have approached life and achievement from many different perspectives and standings. The commonality is that they have achieved success—or, in some cases, achieved the kind of failure that illuminates success in its absence—in their own words and in their own ways. And in almost every case, they worked hard at it.

Success, as I have said, is clearly not material. Often it can only be recognized by its owner. It is not necessarily even fully attainable; it is generally more sought after than achieved. But it is part of an attitudinal achievement level. You should be able to use the definitions and descriptions of success as expressed by other women to illuminate and guide you as you seek your own path.

SUCCESS

"We slowly learn that life consists of processes as well as results, and that failure may come quite as easily from ignoring the adequacy of one's method as from selfish or ignoble aims."

—*JANE ADDAMS*

"If you find it in your heart to care for somebody else, you will have succeeded."

—*MAYA ANGELOU*

"Experience is a good teacher, but she sends in terrific bills."
—*MINNA ANTRIM*

"Perfection consists not in doing extraordinary things, but in doing ordinary things extraordinarily well."
—*ANGELIQUE ARNAULD*

"Everything nourishes what is strong already."
—*JANE AUSTEN*

"For an actress to be a success she must have the face of Venus, the brains of Minerva, the grace of Terpsichore, the memory of Macauley, the figure of Juno and the hide of a rhinoceros."

—*ETHEL BARRYMORE*

"Behind almost every woman you ever heard of stands a man who let her down."

—*NAOMI BLIVEN*

"Act as if it were impossible to fail."

—*DOROTHEA BRANDE*

"Give to the world the best you have, and the best will come back to you."

—*MADELINE BRIDGE*

"Why, dammit, my life's been full to the brim! I've had three babies and raised them; I've got six grandchildren, I've had my health and plenty of work to keep me busy. I loved Harry Brown enough to live under a mesquite bush with him. I've know pain and grief, and lots of happiness and pleasure. What more could a woman ask for?"

—*POLLY HICKS BROWN*

"There were many ways of breaking a heart. Stories were full of hearts broken by love, but what really broke a heart was taking away its dream—whatever that dream might be."

—*PEARL S. BUCK*

"Nature gives you the face you have at twenty; it is up to you to merit the face you have at fifty."

—COCO CHANEL

"If you're in a good profession, it's hard to get bored, because you're never finished, there will always be work you haven't done."

—JULIA CHILD

"Privacy and security are those things you give up when you show the world what makes you extraordinary."

—MARGARET CHO

"We can build upon foundations anywhere if they are well and firmly laid."

—IVY COMPTON-BURNETT

"Your goal should be out of reach but not out of sight."

—ANITA DEFRANTZ

"I thought I could change the world. It took me a hundred years to figure out I can't change the world. I can only change Bessie. And honey, that ain't easy, either."

—BESSIE DELANY

"Fame is a fickle food upon a shifting plate."

—EMILY DICKINSON

"Success is counted sweetest by those who ne'er succeed."
—*EMILY DICKINSON*

"How we spend our days is, of course, how we spend our lives."

—*ANNIE DILLARD*

"A peace which covers all the children of the world is my wish."

—*SHIRIN EBADI*

"Praise and attitude of gratitude are unbeatable stimulators. We increase whatever we extol."
—*SYLVIA STITT EDWARDS*

"All my possessions for a moment of time."
—*QUEEN ELIZABETH I*

"The upward course of a nation's history is due in the long run to the soundness of heart of its average men and women."
—*QUEEN ELIZABETH II*

"It isn't where you came from; it's where you are going that counts."

—*ELLA FITZGERALD*

"We all live with the objective of being happy; our lives are all different and yet the same."

—*ANNE FRANK*

"It is doing, not just being, feeling, or sweeping the floor that gets dirty again, which brings women into history."

—*BETTY FRIEDAN*

"Until liberty is attained—the broadest, the deepest, the highest liberty for all—not one set alone, one clique alone, but for men and women, black and white, Irish, Germans, Americans and Negroes, there can be no permanent peace."

—*MATILDA JOSLYN GAGE*

"Success can only be measured in terms of distance traveled."

—*MAVIS GALLANT*

"The story of love is not important—what is important is that one is capable of love. It is perhaps the only glimpse we are permitted of eternity."

—*HELEN HAYES*

"Success is like reaching an important birthday and finding you're exactly the same."

—*AUDREY HEPBURN*

"You build a reputation by hard work, honoring commitments, keeping promises, being supportive, taking defeats with grace, and practicing trust and love."
—*SHIRLEY HUFSTEDLER*

"The most pathetic person in the world is someone who has sight, but no vision."
—*HELEN KELLER*

"I think success has no rules, but you can learn a great deal from failure."
—*JEAN KERR*

"A champion is afraid of losing. Everyone else is afraid of winning."
—*BILLIE JEAN KING*

"Champions keep playing until they get it right."
—*BILLIE JEAN KING*

"To be successful, the first thing to do is fall in love with your work."
—*SISTER MARY LAURETTA*

"It is good to have an end to journey towards, but it is the journey that matters, in the end."
—*URSULA K. LeGUIN*

"Dying is easy, it's living that scares me to death."
—ANNIE LENNOX

"To be a woman is to have interests and duties, raying out in all directions from the central mother-core, like spokes from the hub of a wheel."
—ANNE MORROW LINDBERGH

"Even the smallest victory is never to be taken for granted. Each victory must be applauded."
—AUDRE LORDE

"The time is now to broaden the understanding of peace: there can be no peace without equitable development; and there can be no development without sustainable management of the environment in a democratic and peaceful space. This shift is an idea whose time has come."
—WANGARI MAATHAI

"Reach for it. Push yourself as far as you can. Reach for the stars."
—CHRISTA MCAULIFFE

"We all live in suspense, from day to day, from hour to hour; in other words, we are the hero of our own story."
—MARY MCCARTHY

"Because of their age-long training in human relations—for that is what feminine intuition really is—women have a special contribution to make to any group enterprise."
—*MARGARET MEAD*

"I didn't belong as a kid, and that always bothered me. If only I'd known that one day my differences would be an asset, then my early life would have been much easier."
—*BETTE MIDLER*

"Fortune does not change men. It unmasks them."
—*SUSANNE CURCHOD NECKER*

"I still want to do my work. I still want to do my livingness. And I have lived. I have been fulfilled. I recognized what I had and I never sold it short. And I ain't through yet."
—*LOUISE NEVELSON*

"When you do something you are proud of, dwell on it a little, praise yourself for it."
—*MILDRED NEWMAN*

"Men fear women's strength."
—*ANAÏS NIN*

"Bad moments, like good ones, tend to be grouped together."
—*EDNA O'BRIEN*

"Do the best you can in every task, no matter how unimportant it may seem at the time. No one learns more about a problem than the person at the bottom."
—*SANDRA DAY O'CONNOR*

"I feel there is something unexplored about woman that only a woman can explore."
—*GEORGIA O'KEEFFE*

"Out of every crisis comes the chance to be reborn, to reconceive ourselves as individuals, to choose the kind of change that will help us to grow and to fulfill ourselves more completely."
—*NENA O'NEILL*

"Oh, life is a glorious cycle of song,
A medley of extemporanea,
And love is a thing that can never go wrong,
And I am Marie of Romania."
—*DOROTHY PARKER*

"If your success is not on your own terms, if it looks good to the world but does not feel good in your heart, it is not success at all."
—*ANNA QUINDLEN*

"Happiness is that state of consciousness which proceeds from the achievement of one's value."
—*AYN RAND*

"You take people as far as they will go, not as far as you would like them to go."

—*JEANNETTE RANKIN*

"The single most impressive fact about the attempt by American women to obtain the right to vote is how long it took."

—*ALICE ROSSI*

"The idea has gained currency that women have often been handicapped not only by a fear of failure—not unknown to men either—but by a fear of success as well."

—*SONYA RUDIKOFF*

"No woman can call herself free until she can choose consciously whether she will or will not be a mother."

—*MARGARET SANGER*

"Wealth without virtue is no harmless neighbor. Blend them and walk the peak of happiness."

—*SAPPHO*

"Each day, and the living of it, has to be a conscious creation in which discipline and order are relieved with some play and some pure foolishness."

—*MAY SARTON*

"Every woman is a human being—one cannot repeat that too often—and a human being must have occupation if he or she is not to become a nuisance to the world."
                                                    —DOROTHY L. SAYERS

"To be somebody, a woman does not have to be more like a man, but has to be more of a woman."
                                                    —DR. SALLY E. SHAYWITZ

"It's worth taking risks because failure isn't a bad thing as long as you learn from it and use it as a step toward eventual success."
                                                    —MARIA SHRIVER

"When pain has been intertwined with love and closeness, it's very difficult to believe that love and closeness can be experienced without pain."
                                                    —GLORIA STEINEM

"You have to focus on what's important to you and go for it. But don't stab people in the back. It poisons your whole life if you're like that. The ultimate goal is to be an interesting, useful, wholesome person. If you're successful on top of that, then you're way ahead of everybody."
                                                    —MARTHA STEWART

"I am one of those who never knows the direction of my journey until I have almost arrived."
                                                    —ANNA LOUISE STRONG

"People seldom see the halting and painful steps by which the most insignificant success is achieved."

—*ANNE SULLIVAN*

"If you don't know how to do something or if something scares you or looks impossible, you're going to work a lot harder, and in the end you're going to be gratified."

—*ANNE SWEENEY*

"I had three goals in my life; to finish school, to take nurse's training and to come back and work among my people, and to write three books."

—*BETTY MAE TIGER JUMPER*

"My own vision for a better world is one where we accept and enjoy the differences between peoples with tolerance and understanding, respecting all creeds and races for their unique contribution to the world."

—*DAME CATHERINE TIZARD*

"I had crossed the line. I was free, but there was no one to welcome me to the land of freedom. I was a stranger in a strange land."

—*HARRIET TUBMAN*

"A successful man is one who makes more money than his wife can spend. A successful woman is one who can find such a man."

—*LANA TURNER*

"When you break the glass ceiling, you get cut."

—*LUPE VALDEZ*

"Sex prejudice, out in the great world, is not simply a palpable barrier. It's a mental block in any woman's design for living."

—*HARRIET VAN HORNE*

"We are not interested in the possibilities of defeat."

—*QUEEN VICTORIA*

"A sobering thought: What if, right at this very moment, I am living up to my full potential?"

—*JANE WAGNER*

"The animals of the world exist for their own reasons. They were not made for humans any more than black people were made for white, or women created for men."

—*ALICE WALKER*

"Success can make you go one of two ways. It can make you a prima donna—or it can smooth the edges, take away the insecurities and let the nice things come out."

—*BARBARA WALTERS*

"The modern world is not given to uncritical admiration. It expects its idols to have feet of clay, and can be reasonably sure that press and camera will report their exact dimensions."

—*BARBARA WARD*

"It is better to be looked over than overlooked."

—*MAE WEST*

"It is easy enough to be pleasant,
When life flows like a song,
But the person worthwhile is the one who will smile,
When everything goes dead wrong."

—*ELLA WHEELER WILCOX*

"Luck is a matter of preparation meeting opportunity."

—*OPRAH WINFREY*

"We all experience 'soul moments' in life—when we see a magnificent sunrise, hear the call of a loon, see the wrinkles in our mother's hands, or smell the sweetness of a baby. During these moments, our body, as well as our brain, resonates as we experience the glory of being a human being."

—*MARION WOODMAN*

"I wake each morning with the thrill of expectation and the joy of being truly alive. And I'm thankful for this day."

—*ANGELA L. WOZNIAK*

"With each new day I put away the past and discover the new beginnings I have been given."

—*ANGELA L. WOZNIAK*

11

WOMEN

*"Women observe subconsciously a thousand little details, without
knowing they are doing so. Their subconscious mind adds these
little things together—and they call the result intuition."*
—AGATHA CHRISTIE

Women have said so much *about* women that it is difficult not
to build an entire book of quotations around just this topic. The
quotations in this chapter are just a sampling of what we have
said about ourselves and each other. They were selected to illuminate and illustrate the variety of those views.

Not surprisingly, many of these quotations exalt women
and women's contributions. Many do so by contrasting—sometimes humorously, sometimes not—women with men. What I
have worked hard *not* to include, although there is a limited
amount of it, are representations of the moaning, "poor me" attitude about the lot and fate of women. Happily, most women
who have something to say also say it with a sense of exhilaration, of expectation, of pride, of determination and, quite often,
of joy.

Much of this exhilaration is because, in large measure,
women have had to define themselves. Women throughout history have had a considerably different view of themselves than
have men, and it has caused us to think a great deal about just
what it means to be a woman. In today's society it has led far too
many of us to decide that it has to mean everything. We have to
be super-mom, super-wife, super-executive, super-chauffeur,
super-cook, super-volunteer, or super-something else. And gen-

erally all at the same time. Somewhere along the way we decided that "super" had to be a prefix for everything that we did.

Isn't it fascinating that women have been perfectly willing to allow men to define themselves in the most tolerant, accepting terms possible, and we have been perfectly willing to accept those definitions? But have we been willing to define ourselves in those same generous terms? Every woman reader knows the answer to that question.

I am always fascinated as I review my collection of quotations at the varying stages of self-definition revealed in the words of these women. Setting aside differences of chronology and place in history, some are still desperately struggling, unwilling or unable to become "un-hyphenated." Many others have made it into a newer, freer reality. There is a place for the words of both groups of women.

As you read these words and perhaps collect quotations of your own, I encourage you to think about your personal progress along this path of self-definition.

Some of us have learned to accept a standard of less-than-perfection, both in ourselves and in other women. Some of us have gotten to the point of "ego-comfort," or self-awareness where we can accept who we are—figurative warts, literal wrinkles and all.

The main thing is to be a person who is imperfect but competent, imperfectible but undaunted, and who can laugh at things either way. Be a woman. Be a real person. That's really all you have to be.

WOMEN

"I do not believe that women are better than men. We have not wrecked railroads, nor corrupted legislatures, nor done many unholy things that men have done; but then we must remember that we have not had the chance."

—*JANE ADDAMS*

"I like to help women help themselves, as that is, in my opinion, the best way to settle the woman question."

—*LOUISA MAY ALCOTT*

"Some people regard discipline as a chore. For me, it is a kind of order that sets me free."

—*JULIE ANDREWS*

"We learn the inner secret of happiness when we learn to direct our inner drives, our interest and our attention to something besides ourselves."

—*ETHEL PERCY ANDRUS*

"The true Republic: men: their rights and nothing more; women: their rights and nothing less."

—*SUSAN B. ANTHONY*

"But the advance of women is not only thanks to the efforts of these pioneers. It is also the result of the endeavors of millions of women and their daily sacrifices on behalf of their families and their children's future; women who often work in difficult conditions, and who are the pillars of our communities. The emancipation of women starts there, in their homes."

—*Michelle Bachelet*

"What is the issue at the core of modern politics? CRE-DI-BI-LI-TY. Talk less, deliver more. There is a direct link between the entry of women into the labor force and the reduction of poverty. Increased participation of women in the workforce is not only crucial for development, it is a moral imperative."

—*Michelle Bachelet*

"Bringing women's views and strengths into public debate, practice, and decision-making everywhere is crucial. A viable future for our earth and its inhabitants depends on it."

—*Susan McGee Bailey*

"The only thing I regret about my past is the length of it. If I had to live my life again, I'd make the same mistakes, only sooner."

—*Tallulah Bankhead*

"The most mediocre of males feels himself a demigod as compared with women."

—*Simone de Beauvoir*

"Female friendships that work are relationships in which women help each other to belong to themselves."

—LOUISE BERNIKOW

"Next to God we are indebted to women, first for life itself, and then for making it worth living."

—MARY MCLEOD BETHUNE

"A woman's head is always influenced by her heart; but a man's heart by his head."

—LADY BLESSINGTON (MARGUERITE POWER GARDINER)

"Forget the past and live the present hour."

—SARAH KNOWLES BOLTON

"When women are depressed they either eat or go shopping. Men invade another country."

—ELAYNE BOOSLER

"People are just not very ambitious for women still. Your son you want to be the best he can be. Your daughter you want to be happy."

—ALEXA CANADY

"Tremendous amounts of talent are being lost to our society just because that talent wears a skirt."

—SHIRLEY CHISHOLM

"Women lead by means of reconciliation, interrelations and persuasion, and bring with them the moral values they learned at home. Men usually lead through control and intimidation. Reconciliation unites people and allows them to work together for the benefit of all."

—*VIOLETA BARRIOS DE CHAMORRO*

"Women are always being tested but, ultimately, each of us has to define who we are individually and then do the very best job we can to grow into that."

—*HILLARY RODHAM CLINTON*

"Sorrow, fear, physical pain, excessive heat and excessive cold. I can still guarantee to stand up to all these with decent courage. But I abdicate in the face of boredom, which turns me into a wretched and, if necessary, ferocious creature."

—*COLETTE*

"We, the Black women of today, must accept the full weight of a legacy wrought in blood by our mothers in chains, as heirs to a tradition of supreme perseverance and heroic resistance."

—*ANGELA DAVIS*

"It is only the women whose eyes have been washed clear with tears who get the broad vision that makes them little sisters to all the world."

—*DOROTHEA DIX*

"When women's true history shall have been written, her part in the upbuilding of this nation will astound the world."

—*ABIGAIL SCOTT DUNIWAY*

"When women are marginalized, Democracy is impossible."

—*SHIRIN EBADI*

"I can spot empty flattery and know exactly where I stand. In the end it's really only my own approval or disapproval that means anything."

—*AGNETHA FALTSKOG*

"Who knows of the possibilities of love when men and women share not only children, home, and garden, not only the fulfillment of their biological roles, but the responsibilities and passions of the work that creates the human future. It has barely begun, the search of women for themselves."

—*BETTY FRIEDAN*

"The especial genius of women, I believe, is to be electrical in movement, intuitive in function, spiritual in tendency."

—*MARGARET FULLER*

"You can never imagine what it is to have a man's force of genius in you and yet to suffer the slavery of being a girl."

—*CAROLYN G. HEILBRUN (AMANDA CROSS)*

"People, even more than things, have to be restored, re-newed, revived, reclaimed, and redeemed; never throw out anyone."

—*AUDREY HEPBURN*

"You're born, you live, you get some terrible disease and get knocked off. I think it's a relief to be alive—if you can enjoy life. And it's a relief to be dead, if you enjoy sleeping."

—*KATHARINE HEPBURN*

"Men seem to kick friendship around like a football, but it doesn't seem to crack. Women treat it as glass and it goes to pieces."

—*ANNE MORROW LINDBERGH*

"Because I am a woman, I must make unusual efforts to suc-ceed. If I fail, no one will say, 'She doesn't have what it takes.' They will say, 'Women don't have what it takes.'"

—*CLARE BOOTHE LUCE*

"The test of a man is how well he is able to feel about what he thinks. The test of a woman is how well she is able to think about what she feels."

—*MARY S. MCDOWELL*

"I do not believe in using women in combat, because fe-males are too fierce."

—*MARGARET MEAD*

"Whether women are better than men I cannot say—but I can say they are certainly no worse."

—*GOLDA MEIR*

"Women and elephants never forget."

—*DOROTHY PARKER*

"A woman has got to love a bad man once or twice in her life to be thankful for a good one."

—*MARJORIE KINNAN RAWLINGS*

"In a society where the rights and potential of women are constrained, no man can be truly free. He may have power, but he will not have freedom."

—*MARY ROBINSON*

"When men talk about defense, they always claim to be protecting women and children, but they never ask women and children what they think."

—*PAT SCHROEDER*

"What is most beautiful in virile men is something feminine; what is most beautiful in feminine women is something masculine."

—*SUSAN SONTAG*

"Resolved: that it is the duty of women of this country to secure to themselves their sacred right to the elective franchise."

—*ELIZABETH CADY STANTON*

"Each arc of colour may be lovely to behold, but it is the full spectrum of our woman rainbow that glows with the brightest promise of better things to come."

—*MERLIN STONE*

"Women are the real architects of society."

—*HARRIET BEECHER STOWE*

"If the first woman God ever made was strong enough to turn the world upside down all alone, these together ought to be able to turn it back and get it right side up again, and now that they're asking to do it, the men better let them."

—*SOJOURNER TRUTH*

"I only like two kinds of men: domestic and imported."

—*MAE WEST*

"When man, governed by reasonable laws, enjoys his natural freedom, let him despise woman, if she do not share it with him."

—*MARY WOLLSTONECRAFT*

BIOGRAPHICAL
INDEX

BIOGRAPHICAL INDEX
(Page numbers follow in italics)

Chisholm, Shirley (1924-2005) African-American congresswoman/first woman presidential candidate, *94, 139*

Cho, Margaret (b. 1968) Korean-American comedienne, *19, 123*

Christie, Agatha (1891-1975) English mystery writer, *66, 135*

Christina, Queen (Kristina Augusta) (1629-1689) queen of Sweden, *19*

Churchill, Jennie Jerome (1854-1921) American-born mother of Winston Churchill, *5, 19*

Clarke, Susan (1959-2006) American journalist, *108*

Clifton, Lucille (b. 1936) African-American author/poet, *5*

Clinton, Hillary Rodham (b. 1947) American first lady/senator/secretary of state, *56, 82, 95, 140*

Cochran, Jacqueline (1910-1980) American pilot, *108*

Cole, Johnetta B. (b. 1936) African-American educator, *19, 56*

Colette (1873-1954) French author, *66, 140*

Collins, Eileen (b. 1956) American astronaut, *83*

Collins, Judy (b. 1939) American folk singer, *108*

Compton-Burnett, Ivy (1884-1969) English author, *123*

Cook, Mary Lou (b. 1910) American artist, *5*

Curie, Marie (1867-1934) Polish scientist/author/educator, *36*

D

Davis, Angela (b. 1944) African-American activist, *36, 140*

Davis, Belva (b. 1932) African-American activist, *108*

Davis, Bette (1908-1989) American actress, *66*

DeFrantz, Anita (b. 1952) African-American Olympic athlete/attorney, *123*

DeGeneres, Ellen (b. 1958) American comedienne, *66*

Delany, Bessie (1891-1995) African-American dentist/author, *123*

Del Rio, Delores (1905-1983) Mexican film actress, *110*

De Mille, Agnes (1905-1993) American choreographer, *5*

Deming, Barbara (1917-1984) American activist/author, *37*

Diana, Princess of Wales (Lady Spencer) (1961-1997) British princess, *67, 109*

Dickinson, Emily (1830-1886) American poet, *19, 47, 56, 109, 123, 124*

Dietrich, Marlene (1901-1992) German actress/singer, *66*

Difranco, Ani (b. 1970) American folk singer, *5, 56*

Dillard, Annie (b. 1945) American author, *5, 20, 124*

Diller, Phyllis (b. 1917) American comedienne, *67*

Dix, Dorothea (1802-1887) American nurse/social reformer, *140*

McCormick, Anne O'Hare (1882-1954) American journalist, *97*

McDowell, Mary S. (1876-1955) American educator, *142*

McMillan, Terry (b. 1951) African-American author, *114*

Mead, Margaret (1901-1978) American anthropologist/author, *39, 53, 73, 97, 128, 142*

Meir, Golda (1898-1978) Israeli prime minister, *26, 97, 143*

Midler, Bette (b. 1945) American actress/singer, *73, 128*

Millay, Edna St. Vincent (1892-1950) American poet, *26*

Mitford, Nancy (1905-1973) English satirist/author, *73, 97*

Monroe, Marilyn (1926-1962) American actress, *73*

Montessori, Maria (1870-1952) Italian educator, *26, 87*

Morrison, Toni (b. 1931) African-American author/winner of Nobel Prize for Literature, *9, 26, 39, 98*

Moses, Grandma (Anna Mary Robertson) (1860-1961) American folk artist, *10*

Murdoch, Iris (1919-1999) English philosopher/author, *1, 39*

Murray, Judith Sargent (1751-1820) American women's rights advocate and writer, *50*

Myrdal, Alva (1902-1986) Swedish socialist/politician/winner of Nobel Peace Prize, *87*

N

Neal, Patricia (b. 1926) American actress, *39*

Necker, Susanne Curchod (1739-1794) Swiss author, prominent in French literary circles, *128*

Nevelson, Louise (1899-1988) American artist, *128*

Nevill, Lady Dorothy (1826-1913) English author, *27*

Newman, Mildred (1920-2001) American psychologist, *128*

Nikoi, Gloria (b. 1930) Ghanaian foreign minister, *98*

Nin, Anaïs (1903-1977) French poet/lecturer, *103, 128*

Norman, Marsha (b. 1947) American playwright, *114*

Norris, Kathleen (b. 1947) American essayist, *10*

Norton, Eleanor Holmes (b. 1937) African-American District of Columbia delegate/member of U.S. Congress, *85, 98*

Novello, Antonia Coello (b. 1944) Puerto Rican-American U.S. surgeon general, *40, 98, 115*

O

Obama, Michelle (b. 1964) African-American first lady/attorney, *27, 114*

O'Brien, Edna (b. 1930) Irish author, *128*

O'Connor, Sandra Day (b. 1930) American jurist/first woman justice of the U.S. Supreme Court, *v, 59, 87, 129*

O'Keeffe, Georgia (1887-1986) American artist, *10, 129*

O'Neill, Nena (1924-2006) American author, *129*

Ono, Yoko (b. 1933) Japanese-American artist, *73*

Ouida, Maria Louise Rame (1839-1908) English novelist, *27*

P

Pagels, Elaine (b. 1943) American educator, *43*

Pankhurst, Emmeline (1858-1928) English suffragist, *87, 98*

Parker, Dorothy (1893-1967) American humorist/writer/poet, *40, 59, 73, 74, 129, 143*

Parks, Rosa (1913-2005) African-American civil rights activist, *27*

Parton, Dolly (b. 1946) American singer/songwriter/actress, *27, 74, 114*

Paul, Alice (1885-1977) American suffragist leader, *87*

Pauley, Jane (b. 1950) American broadcast journalist, *59*

Pavlova, Anna (1881-1931) Russian prima ballerina, *10, 50*

Pearl, Minnie (Sarah Ophelia Colley Cannon) (1912-1996) American entertainer, *74*

Pelosi, Nancy (b. 1940) American congresswoman/first woman speaker of U.S. House of Representatives, *59, 99*

Petry, Ann (1908-1997) African-American author, *74*

Pfeiffer, Michelle (b. 1958) American actress, *59*

Piaf, Edith (1915-1963) French singer, *115*

Piercy, Marge (b. 1936) American author, *115*

Ponder, Catherine (b. 1927) American minister, *27, 74*

Porter, Katherine Anne (1890-1980) American author, *10, 40*

Post, Emily (1872-1960) American author/etiquette expert, *27*

Potter, Beatrix (1866-1943) English children's author/illustrator, *50*

Powell, Alma (b. 1937) African-American audiologist, *115*

Prothrow-Stith, Deborah (b. 1954) African-American physician/educator, *99*

Q

Quindlen, Anna (b. 1953) American columnist/author, *10, 40, 99, 115, 129*

Quinn, Jane Bryant (b. 1939) American journalist, *88*

ACKNOWLEDGMENTS

Since this is a compilation of quotations, I would be tempted to repeat in these Acknowledgments the entire Index because, were it not for the women whose words and thoughts make up this book, there wouldn't be one. Because that idea is impractical, to say the least, there are others, named and unnamed, to whom credit is due:

- to my grandmother, Nellie Hershey Tullis, and my mother, Mary Tullis Rexroat, who were my first teachers, inspirers, and role models;

- to my dear friend, Geraldine Emmett, who, in her ninety-fifth year of life, continues to give me caring and constant encouragement;

- to my children—Cathy, Caron, Steven, Connie, Christopher, and Christi—who have so generously supported my work and almost never asked, "You're doing *what?*";

- to all the women—known and unknown, published and unpublished—who have said and written words of consequence;

- to the women leaders and the women's leadership organizations, including the YWCA of the USA, International Women's Forum, Women's Campaign Fund, National Women's Political Caucus, EMILY's List, Emerge, League of Women Voters, American Association of University Women, Center for Women Policy Studies, Wellesley Center for Research on Women, Stephens College, Stennis Center Summit of Southern Women Leaders, P.E.O., Charter 100, and many others that have encouraged women to think beyond the present and aspire beyond the current;

- to the hundreds of print magazines, journals, newspapers, reference and related publications ranging from *Vital Speeches* to *Women of China* magazine, and Internet sources such as ThinkExist.com and Brainyquote.com, from whose pages a portion of this material and documentation has been confirmed or derived; to the libraries who preserve and protect the written word; and to the librarians who so patiently and skillfully make it available;

- to the good people at Newmarket Press—especially Esther Margolis and my kind and compassionate editor, Keith Hollaman—who think enough of women and their words to publish this book, and to my agent, Suzanne Dowling, whose creativity made the match; and, finally,

- to a special group of friends and colleagues who have encouraged and assisted me so ably in this effort, especially Alta Hulfachor, Bethany Holder, Cyndi Bergerhofer, Rebecca Pepple (my granddaughter), and my business partner of over twenty years, David Bolger.

My gratitude for this book belongs to all of these. The ultimate responsibility for any errors—of omission or commission—is mine alone.

ABOUT THE EDITOR

Carolyn Warner is founder and president of Corporate//Education Consulting, Inc. Drawing on her vast experience in government, business, education, and communications, her firm offers consulting, speaking, seminar, and training services focusing on workforce/workplace issues, education, leadership, and public/private partnerships. Warner is an acclaimed public speaker, delivering more than fifty keynote or seminar presentations annually. Her speaking career—which generated her lifelong fascination with quotations (from both women and men)—stems from her early history as a teenage political "stump speaker" and national award-winning high school debater. She estimates that her collection now exceeds 40,000 separate quotations.

Warner served for twelve years as Arizona's elected State Superintendent of Public Instruction, the first non-educator ever to hold that post. In 1986, she was her party's nominee for Governor, narrowly losing in a three-way general election.

She is the author of the bestseller *The Last Word: A Treasury of Women's Quotes* and also two books on strengthening the connection between schools and communities.

Active on both state and national levels as a respected public policy commentator and education advocate, Warner has received numerous Presidential and Congressional appointments. She currently serves on a number of national boards and commissions, including Jobs for America's Graduates, of which she is National Treasurer, and the Phoenix School of Law.

To contact Carolyn Warner, please e-mail her at info@CarolynWarner.com.

THE ACCLAIMED NEWMARKET *WORDS OF* SERIES

The Words of Extraordinary Women
Selected and Introduced by Carolyn Warner
A celebration of the most important female voices in history, this uplifting and thought-provoking compendium features quotes from notable women on the arts, education, success, and politics; 176 pages.

The Words of Abraham Lincoln
Selected and Introduced by Larry Shapiro
A collection of wise and inspiring quotations from the speeches and writings of Abraham Lincoln covering the slavery controversy, the Civil War, and his personal life. Includes photographs, chronology; 128 pages.

The Words of Albert Schweitzer
Selected and Introduced by Norman Cousins
An inspiring collection focusing on: Knowledge and Discovery, Reverence for Life, Faith, The Life of the Soul, The Musician as Artist, and Civilization and Peace. Includes photographs, chronology, excerpt from acceptance speech for the 1954 Nobel Peace Prize; 112 pages.

The Words of Desmond Tutu
Selected and Introduced by Naomi Tutu
Nearly 100 memorable quotations from the addresses, sermons, and writings of South Africa's Nobel Prize–winning archbishop. Topics include: Faith and Responsibility, Apartheid, Family, Violence and Nonviolence, The Community—Black and White, and Toward a New South Africa. Includes photographs, chronology, text of acceptance speech for the 1984 Nobel Peace Prize; 112 pages.

The Words of Gandhi
Selected and Introduced by Sir Richard Attenborough
More than 150 selections from the letters, speeches, and writings, collected in five sections—Daily Life, Cooperation, Nonviolence, Faith, and Peace. Includes *Time* magazine's millennium essay on Gandhi's impact on the twentieth century; photographs, chronology, bibliography, glossary; 128 pages

The Words of Martin Luther King, Jr.
Selected and Introduced by Coretta Scott King
More than 120 quotations and excerpts from the great civil rights leader's speeches, sermons, and writings on: The Community of Man, Racism, Civil Rights, Justice and Freedom, Faith and Religion, Nonviolence, and Peace. Includes photographs, chronology, text of presidential proclamation of King holiday; 128 pages

The Words of Peace
Selections from the Speeches of the Winners of the Nobel Peace Prize
Selected and Edited by Professor Irwin Abrams. Foreword by President Jimmy Carter
A new compendium of excerpts from award winners' acceptance speeches spanning 1901 to 2007, including Al Gore, the Dalai Lama, Mother Teresa, Lech Walesa, Martin Luther King, Jr., and Elie Wiesel. Themes are: Peace, Human Rights, Violence and Nonviolence, The Bonds of Humanity, and Faith and Hope. Includes photographs, biographical notes, chronology, and index; 176 pages.

Newmarket Press books are available from your local or online bookseller or from Newmarket Press, Special Sales Department, 18 East 48th Street, New York, NY 10017; phone 212-832-3575 or 800-669-3903; fax 212-832-3629; e-mail info@newmarketpress.com. Prices and availability are subject to change. Catalogs and information on quantity order discounts are available on request.

www.newmarketpress.com